PAUL ROBESON

All-American

PAUL ROBESON
All-American

DOROTHY BUTLER GILLIAM

THE NEW REPUBLIC BOOK COMPANY, INC.

Washington, D.C.

Published in 1976 by
The New Republic Book Company, Inc.
1220 Nineteenth St., N.W., Washington, D.C. 20036

Library of Congress Cataloging in Publication Data

Gilliam, Dorothy Butler.
  Paul Robeson, All-American.

  Includes bibliographical references and index.
  1. Robeson, Paul, 1898-1976. I. Title.
E185.97.R638   790.2'092'4 [B]   76-23233
ISBN 0-915220-15-6

Printed in the United States of America

*For Sam, with loving thanks for his understanding and patience,
and to my mother, Jessie Butler, whose faith never wavered.*

Contents

ILLUSTRATIONS

Preface

In 1973, when the *Washington Post* asked me to write Paul Robeson's lengthy obituary (to be put away and used upon his death), my research convinced me that I wanted to write his biography. Robeson's eradication from history had been quite effective; I wanted to know more—I had to know more—about the man who rose from a poor preacher's son to millionaire theatrical, screen, and concert star, and whose political beliefs caused him to be scorned and humiliated in later years. In the 1930s and early 1940s Robeson was a kind of unifying force, a symbolic black who could help heal racial wounds of the past with his artistry and his dedication to universal brotherhood. A few years later his statements that it was "unthinkable" that black Americans could "take up arms in the name of an Eastland to go against anybody," his unwavering leftwing sympathies, had led to the loss of his passport and signaled his artistic death.

How did Robeson become the focus of these complicated social, political, and theatrical forces? What had been the roots of his political stands, the appeal of his performances? To answer these questions, I sought to place Robeson in the context of his times, to see him, as Earl Schenck Miers once suggested in *The Nation*, as more all-American in his adult life "than he was as a member of his college football team."

This is an unauthorized biography. When I approached Robeson's son Paul, Jr., in mid-1974, and told him I wanted to write a book, his answer was that he would neither help nor hinder my efforts. I considered giving up the project then, but a few weeks of intensive preliminary digging convinced me that there was a great deal of material available on Paul Robeson, and the publicly supported Paul Robeson Archives in New York City was open to me. Some persons declined to talk to me, explaining they felt obligated to talk only to the authorized biographer. But countless others did consent to interviews on their knowledge of Robeson's career and their personal association with him.

I interviewed dozens of people whose memories of Robeson had not been tapped by the few earlier Robeson writers, and I had the use of documents such as the portion of the files of the Federal Bureau of Investigation obtainable without family sanction under the Freedom of Information Act.

I am sincerely sorry that I cannot name each person who contributed to the writing of this book. But I must express my deep gratitude for the assistance I was given by an extraordinary editor, Leon King, now a senior editor of Schocken Books. Mr. King gave important advice and asked relevant questions, all the while maintaining an equilibrium that was most assuring. I would like to thank, too, a fine editor, Joan Tapper, of New Republic Books, for the dynamic quality of her assistance and her gentle guidance over the hazardous traps that can befall a first author. I want to express appreciation to Thomas R. Kendrick of *The Washington Post*, my secretary, Nancy Frost, and in addition to salaried researchers, two unpaid research assistants— Rother C. Owens in America and Robert E. Hood in Europe—who helped because they thought the cause merited it. A final acknowledgment is due Marie Seton, who wrote a Robeson biography nearly twenty years ago and allowed me to quote material for which she is the only source. Ms. Seton read the manuscript, made important suggestions, and gave a strong nod of encouragement at a crucial stage in the book's preparation.

Washington, D.C.   DOROTHY GILLIAM
July 1976

"*As a product of his times Robeson today is perhaps more all-American than he was as a member of his college football team.*"

—Earl Schenck Miers in
The Nation, 1950

Prologue

April 15, 1973. A capacity audience crowded into Carnegie Hall, drawn, despite the afternoon's unseasonable briskness, to a "cultural salute" to the seventy-fifth birthday of Paul Robeson. They came to see highlights of a career that spanned sports, law school, theater, concert hall, and political forums. They came to hear the reminiscences of actors like Zero Mostel and Sidney Poitier, the songs of Harry Belafonte and Pete Seeger, the tributes of former Attorney General Ramsey Clark, Mrs. Martin Luther King, Jr., and Angela Davis, the telegraphed messages of heads of state.

Robeson himself was absent. He was ill and in seclusion. The audience—of all ages, races, and political persuasions, like the audiences who thronged to him during the years of popularity and controversy—would hear only his recorded message crackling through the cavernous hall: "I want you to know that I am the same Paul, dedicated as ever to the worldwide cause of humanity for freedom, peace, and brotherhood."

It was a message that had unified a disparate group of sponsors—artists, civil-rights activists, fragments of the scattered Old Left—behind the Birthday Committee Chairman, lawyer Hope Stevens: Among the organizers of the event were people as varied as Lillian Hellman, Dizzy Gillespie, Judge George W. Crockett, Jr., and Bishop J. Clinton Hoggard, Woody Allen and Gregory Peck, Leonard Bernstein and Diahann Carroll, Gunnar Myrdal and Ring Lardner, Jr., labor leader Harry Bridges and publisher Angus Cameron. Said one New York lawyer, "I can't think of anyone else who could have done it."

Yet Robeson's life story, which so often crystallized the social and artistic movements of the twentieth century—the Negro Renaissance of the 1920s, the political awareness of the 1930s, the Allied solidarity of World War II, the hysterical backlash of McCarthyism—had all but disappeared from the public consciousness. His name had faded from the pages of the daily newspaper when this giant of a black man returned from self-imposed exile in the early 1960s and retired to his sister's house in Philadelphia. This day in April would mark a rekindled interest in Robeson's huge talent, in his electric personality.

It was left to his son, Paul Robeson, Jr., to put the significance of the Salute into words: "This day is a moment of great triumph. It has torn to shreds the curtain of silence that had been drawn around my father. Now the way is open for an entire generation of Americans to see (him) in the light of today."

I:

Father and Son

Princeton, New Jersey, around the turn of the century, was a quiet, genteel town rather smugly proud of its long history, its charming landscape, and its college, which was in transition from, as one observer put it, "a highclass country club to a real university."[1] The town received its name in 1724, probably in honor of William III of England and Prince of Orange-Nassau, some fifty years after farmers, mostly Quakers, had settled in the area. Thirty years later, with an appropriation of land and money from the town, the eight-year-old College of New Jersey moved from Newark to Princeton, and by 1756 it was holding classes in Nassau Hall, the largest public building in the colonies. From then on the college and the town played an important part in the history of the nation. John Witherspoon, president of the college, and Richard Stockton, the town's most prominent resident, both signed the Declaration of Independence. The Battle of Princeton was a decisive event in the Revolutionary War; and Princeton was the temporary capital of the country in 1783, when Congress, meeting at Nassau Hall, received word that the Treaty of Paris had ended the war.

As the years passed, Princeton responded to the new forces that were stimulating the new nation's growth. Before the war it had been an important way-stop on the New York-Philadelphia stage line, noted for its famous inns on Nassau Street; in the 1830s, when the Delaware and Raritan Canal and the Camden and Amboy Railroad were completed, it became a bustling transportation center with some industry. But the removal of the railroad tracks to Princeton Junction during the Civil War quickly changed its character. Princeton became a tranquil town, dominated economically and socially by the college. In 1896, on its 150th anniversary, the College of New Jersey became Princeton University. Its course for the future was set by Professor

Woodrow Wilson's phrase during the ceremonies, "Princeton in the nation's service."

The poorer section of Princeton, the black community, was, as a writer commented as late as 1921, "almost totally unknown to the casual visitor" in the town. "No street runs from this section to the west end of town where the best residences of Princeton are located."[2] The Negro section was bounded by Nassau Street on the south, John Street on the east, and Witherspoon Street on the west, which as early as 1804 was already being called "African Lane," although some of the town's oldest families lived on the street until well into the nineteenth century. Toward the end of the century Witherspoon, Green, Quarry, Hulfish, John, and the other streets in the area were still unpaved, but they were dotted with modest homes and churches, which served as religious and social centers for the community.

The separation between blacks and whites in Princeton was almost as rigid as in the South. The person who moved most freely between the two groups was the black preacher, his community's emissary and its shaky bridge across the chasm of segregation. For some twenty years that man was William Drew Robeson.

He was a dark-skinned man of average height, broad shoulders, and classic African features, who for the first fifteen years after his birth on July 27, 1845, had lived in a one-room cabin without windows on a plantation near Raleigh, North Carolina. In 1860, on the eve of the Civil War, he ran away from the plantation, leaving behind his parents. A year later he had joined the legions of other blacks fighting in the Union army. After the war William settled in Pennsylvania. It was a likely place for a young former slave to get an education. As early as 1854, the Presbyterian-sponsored all-black Ashmun Institute, named for Jehudi Ashmun, the reorganizer of the colony of Liberia, had received its charter from the Pennsylvania Legislature and admitted its first students. Located in Chester County, about forty-five miles from Philadelphia (because the white founders wanted a rural site "freed from the distractions which beset the colored student in city life"), the Institute changed its name to Lincoln University in 1866. Five years later the theological department was placed under the supervision of the Presbyterian Church, with a three-year program open to students who had "passed through a course of classical and scientific study." By 1872-1873 William was a senior in the classical program, taking courses such as Latin and ancient history.[3] It was while he was in the theological program that he met Maria Louisa Bustill, a tall, slender woman with pale brown eyes, whose olive skin and raven hair suggested the mixture of African, Cherokee Indian, and white Quaker blood that flowed in her veins.

Bustill family roots go deep into American soil. Maria's great-great-grandfather, Cyrus Bustill, born in Burlington, New Jersey, in 1732, purchased his freedom before the Revolution and joined the sizable community of free blacks in Philadelphia, where he worked as a baker. During the Revolutionary War he supplied the rebels and received thanks from George Washington for the bread he delivered to the starving troops at Valley Forge. In 1787 he helped to establish the Free African Society of Philadelphia.

Joseph C. Bustill, Maria's grandfather, was an agent for the Underground Railroad and helped over a thousand fugitive slaves to freedom. He also founded the First Colored Presbyterian Church of Harrisburg, Pennsylvania. Early Bustills included riverboat captains and artists and later generations became teachers and for years taught in the public schools of Philadelphia. Maria, born in Philadelphia on November 8, 1853, and her sister Gertrude followed this tradition.

William and Maria were married on July 11, 1878. After he received his theology degree William became the pastor of a community in Wilkes-Barre, Pennsylvania, but in 1879 he was called to the Witherspoon Street Presbyterian Church in Princeton, New Jersey. His congregation was swelled by blacks who migrated from the South in search of better opportunities. Like thousands of others after the Civil War and during the violent collapse of Reconstruction they went to communities where friends and relatives had settled, in a pattern followed by many of William's kinfolk as well. The black community in Princeton was small and poor, and many of the members of the Witherspoon Presbyterian Church came to rely heavily on Reverend Robeson as their leader. Whether recent arrival or older resident, there was often little recourse but to appeal to wealthy white largesse when help was needed for any unusual activity or simply to make ends meet. As pastor of his church, William acted as the mediator between his congregation and the town; so for some twenty years before Paul was born, he solicited money when his flock needed it and interceded in problems that affected the black community at large. Robeson often went hat in hand, but his broad shoulders never slumped and, Paul recalled later, "even the most lordly of aristocratic Princeton had to respect him."[4]

The parsonage provided for the pastor of Witherspoon was located at 72 Witherspoon Street. Here, William and Maria set up housekeeping and started to raise their family. In 1881 Maria gave birth to their first child, named William Drew, Jr., after his father. Another son, Reeve (called Reed), was born five years later; a third, Benjamin, born six years after that, was followed in two years by Marion, the only girl. Then, on April 9, 1898, when the town was draped with orange and black banners as Princeton men marched off to the Spanish-American War, the last of the Robeson children was born. A fat, cheerful baby, he was named Paul Leroy.

The middle-aged couple was bringing their youngest son into an America in which darkly portentous developments were unfolding for the nation's blacks. The failure of Reconstruction had brought violent racial hatreds in its wake, especially in the South where lynchings, Jim Crow laws, and the semislavery of tenant farming became a way of life. In 1896 Jim Crow laws in travel and in all areas of public life were given official sanction by the Supreme Court's decision in *Plessy* v. *Ferguson*. A year earlier Booker T. Washington, in his famous Atlanta Exposition Address, called for conciliation and gradualism while advocating industrial education and social separation for blacks. Washington was praised by many whites, who thought he was the "greatest thing since Lee," and he won the support of many blacks as well. But not all. Black intellectuals reacted with indignation. Monroe Trotter, the first black elected Phi Beta Kappa at Harvard, branded Washington a traitor to the race. And in 1903 W. E. B. Du Bois, a member of the faculty of Atlanta University who in 1895 had become the first black to earn a doctorate at Harvard, devoted a chapter of *The Souls of Black Folk* to Washington's philosophy, which he said put the blame and the onus for reform on the blacks, who were really the victims, not the perpetrators.

Wherever he stood politically between Booker T. Washington and W. E. B. Du Bois, in practice he adhered to the latter's view that a talented tenth, college-educated intellectuals, would have to advance the race and lift up their more oppressed brethren. Washington's vocational education approach was not for the Robeson children, and the pastor insisted that they learn the classics—Latin, philosophy, history, and literature. A man of great dignity, a stern but loving father, whose ruling passion was that his children fulfill their maximum potential and never measure their achievements against those of others, he constantly urged them to "aim high." Maria, the perfect minister's wife, cared for her family, tended the sick, and even wrote some of her husband's sermons. Over the years cataracts gradually clouded her vision, but this seemed only to heighten her spiritual awareness and increase the aura of warmth and comfort she gave to the household.

When Paul was quite young, two misfortunes overtook the Robesons, changing irrevocably the family's lifestyle. Reverend Robeson suffered the first terrible blow. In 1899, when Paul was about a year old, his father was ousted from the pulpit of the Witherspoon Presbyterian Church in a dispute never fully explained. Paul later wrote that it was the result of "a factional dispute among the members. . ." and "that some of his closest kin were part of the ousting faction."[5] Robeson family friends vehemently denied a newspaper report of many years later that the minister was removed because of a female member of his congregation. Given the intense political infighting within denominations, any number of factors may have caused his removal. Whatever the reason, it must have been a terrible trauma for the proud, dignified man who had worked hard to become a minister and who had been the respected leader of his community for twenty years. But William Robeson could not afford the luxury of self-pity and recrimination. He moved his family from the parsonage to a modest two-story frame house at 13 Green Street, hard by the dirt road. Then he got a horse and wagon and went to work hauling ashes for the well-to-do. One of Paul's most vivid early memories was of his father gently guiding their mare, Bess, home with the wagon and of the mound of ashes growing ever higher in back of their house on Green Street. Maria Robeson was as stunned by her husband's fall as he was himself. But theirs was a family where the deepest feelings often weren't expressed in words, so it was by example that she expressed her feelings of love and family solidarity. Then, three months before Paul's sixth birthday, the cataracts on his mother's eyes caused a second tragedy.

On a cold January day in 1904, Maria and twelve-year-old Ben were cleaning the house. As Maria lifted the iron stove in the living room by the front legs, just enough for Ben to pull away the carpet that lay beneath, a hot coal fell from the sliding door, setting fire to her long dress. Nearly blind, she did not see the coal and only felt the blaze when it began scorching her feet and legs. Ben desperately tried to help her beat the flames out of her skirt, but the fire kept spreading. He ran for help. When William Robeson returned home later that day, he found his wife critically burned and being tended by neighbors. She died soon after.

Now William Robeson would have to be both father and mother to
his children. Bill, the oldest, was already at Lincoln University, but that
left four children for the Reverend to manage alone. It would be
difficult, yet he was determined that nothing should stop them from
getting an education. He scraped together the money and sent Ben to
prep school and Biddle (now Johnson C. Smith) University in North
Carolina. Marion went to Scotia Seminary, a school for black girls, also
in North Carolina. This left only two children at home, young Paul
and, for a while, Reed.

Of all of the children only Reed failed to meet the Reverend's
expectations, and in fact disappointed him deeply, although Paul said
Bill never fulfilled his potential either. Rough and carefree, Reed
worked as a hack driver for Princeton's students. He was fiercely
defiant, and if he heard a student say something that was racially
insulting, he would not hesitate to leap down from his coachman's seat
and pummel him, or to use the little bag of jagged rocks he carried. The
Princeton police were constantly picking Reed up. Then the Reverend
Robeson would have to travel downtown to get him out of trouble.
Finally, about 1906, the elder Robeson asked his son to leave home.
The boy's defiance could cost him his life, and it was a bad example for
the youngest child. Nevertheless, for Paul, who had always looked up
to his strong-willed older brother, it was a difficult separation.

This left Paul alone with his father, a man of advanced age with the
still-pronounced air of a dignified preacher. William Robeson's natural
reserve made it difficult for him to express outwardly the deep love he
had for his son, yet he mothered the boy, attending to his comfort and
instilling in him a sense of security. Ever concerned about his
children's education, he coached young Paul in diction and saw that his
time was blocked out and filled in with lessons to learn and books to
read. For his part, Paul would sit with him for hours playing checkers,
and he loved to walk down Green, Hulfish, and Quarry Streets hand in
hand with the old man. Paul loved his father "like no one in all the
world,"[6] although as a young man he would later regret that his
childhood was so programmed. "If I had had time . . . that wasn't
blocked out and filled in for me, I think my imagination would have
been more developed. As it is, I've almost none. All my time was
crowded with lessons to learn, games to play, books to read. I never
can remember having had hours in which I had nothing to do, and had
actually to entertain myself out of my own mind."[7]

Nevertheless, he always looked forward to the summer, when his
sister and brothers would come home on vacations. He would play

football with Ben, who would show him how to throw a pass, how to block and tackle. Bill, the brain of the family, taught him how to question what he read, how to draw his own conclusions, and how to defend them. And then there was Marion, who intended to become a teacher like her mother. Strong-willed but cheerful, she always brought laughter to the household.

Paul's mothering was not confined to his home. Across the street and down each block were aunts and uncles and cousins and some "relatives" who weren't really related. In a sense the whole of Negro Princeton helped to raise the boy. He always had a place at their tables or a bed for the night. When Reverend Robeson, who also drove a hack to make ends meet, had to drive Princeton students on overnight outings, he never worried as his carriage clicked sharply away from Princeton's stone streets. He knew there was always a place for the lad at the home of a friend or neighbor.

Young Paul did not quite understand why, but from the time he was very small, Princeton's blacks had a special feeling for him. Many thought he was destined for great things. The women rocking on their little wood-frame porches would tell him, "You'll grow up to be a credit to us, you'll see."

But Paul, somber-eyed, his close-cropped hair brushed stiffly to the side, a head taller than many of his playmates even then, would barely cast a backward glance at them as he raced away to play Follow the Leader, Mumblety-Peg, or baseball in the weed-infested lots. Part of his specialness, he must have sensed, was directed toward his father, and that "something deep down inside" did not keep him from leaving the old people to wander to a vacant lot where, eyes scrunched up against the sun, he would knock his baseball as far as he could across the open field.

When Paul was nine, Reverend Robeson decided to move to Westfield, New Jersey, where he felt he could earn more money. He found a job in a grocery and living space for himself and Paul in the back above the storeroom. The quarters were small, and when the other children came home for summer vacation they had to sleep several to a bed. But there were advantages. In Westfield Paul attended a racially mixed grammar school, because there were too few Negro children to warrant building a separate black school.

A few months after the move, moreover, Reverend Robeson returned to preaching. By now he was sixty-two, but the chance to go back to his calling, even though in the beginning his congregation was made up of only a dozen members, infused him with youthful vigor. He set about building a new church—the Downing Street African Methodist Episcopal Zion Church—for he had joined a different denomination.

Paul's growing up in Westfield was punctured by stories of racial violence. The myth that it was mainly a southern phenomenon was exploded when, one August day in 1908, his father was shaken to hear of the riot in Springfield, Illinois. A white woman had accused a Negro of beating her, a story she later changed. But white passions were aroused, and when the blood finally was mopped from the street, a couple of miles from Abraham Lincoln's grave, two blacks had been lynched, four white men had been killed, and over seventy persons had been hurt. To outraged but powerless blacks, it seemed that the predictions of W. E. B. Du Bois five years earlier would come true: The problem of color would be the decisive one of the twentieth century.

In 1910, when Paul was twelve, the Robesons left Westfield for Somerville, New Jersey, where Reverend Robeson became pastor of St. Thomas A.M.E. Zion Church. Somerville was larger than either Princeton or Westfield and did not have Princeton's rigid caste system and southern ambience. Nor was the black community as close physically or emotionally as it was in Princeton. Here the Robesons were the only blacks on the street. Nevertheless, there was a separate elementary school for colored children. A one-story, two-room, frame building, it was run by James L. Jamison, a man whose back bore the welts of lashings he had received in the South, when he defied plantation owners and kept his school open during cotton-picking time.

Though Paul was a friendly, outgoing adolescent, he knew the loneliness of a boy without a mother. In Princeton the loneliness had been muted by the close-knit black community. In Somerville it was more poignant, though Paul had a number of friends. He often played with Sam Woldin, the slim, white boy who lived across the street from him, and he was popular among his classmates at Jamison's school. One of his special friends was Margaret Potter, whom he taught to ice skate and whose mother often invited him to dinner.

In 1912 Paul graduated from Jamison's school at the head of his class and entered Somerville High School. One of three blacks among some 250 pupils, Paul was one of the eight students who carried a classical load—Latin, German, math, English, chemistry, physics, and ancient history. Many of the teachers went out of their way to make him feel welcome. Anna Miller, his English teacher, coached him in speaking and debating. Miss Bagg, who taught chemistry and physics, urged him to attend the school parties and dances and, when he did, always danced with him first. But Paul, who was not one to push himself forward, turned down most of these invitations because he felt that something unpleasant might happen. He felt a special responsibility to "act right," to do nothing that would give the whites cause to fear him.

Paul lost no time in establishing himself as an exceptional student, outstanding in sports as well as other activities. As a ninth and tenth grader he became known throughout the area for his abilities in football, playing several different positions, if necessary. He could get the team five or six yards playing fullback, then throw a ball seventy yards—two thirds of the field. One year he played so hard that he broke his collar bone.

He was also Somerville's prize debater. "He was the cleanup man, the third speaker. We used him for rebuttal," recalled Douglas Brown, one of his white classmates who later became a dean at Princeton. During one debate, in opposition to proposed national legislation that would have required immigrants to be able to read and write, Paul rose and "made the audience weep, by reciting the lines from the Statue of Liberty," said Brown. He was so effective that the next time they opposed the same team, the debaters requested them not to introduce any sentiment. Somerville lost. They were very good on sentiment.

Then there was the dramatic club. Once when Doug Brown and Paul were cast respectively as Brutus and Marc Antony in *Julius Caesar,* the two boys decided to infuse the play with some unanticipated reality. They made a dummy corpse of Caesar, put it on a stretcher, splashed catsup across it, and then covered the corpse with a sheet. During the play, when Marc Antony intoned: "The noble Brutus has told you that Caesar is ambitious . . . if you have tears prepare to shed them now," Paul whipped off the sheet and exposed a "beautiful display of gore," Brown remembered.[8] The students loved it, but the drama coach was livid.

And always there was music. Paul had loved music since he was a little boy, when in his father's church he heard hymns and spirituals that became a part of his life. At the frequent church socials when every child was called on to do something, most of the Robeson children recited poems. But Paul usually sang. Later, he helped with the choir. As he got older, his talent attracted a little attention. The music teacher of Somerville High took a special interest in his voice and made Paul soloist of the glee club.

Paul was very popular at Somerville High. As the son of the

respected Reverend Robeson, and a model athlete and student, even his white classmates' parents welcomed him to their homes. One of the few exceptions to this climate of superficial acceptance was evidenced by Somerville's principal, Dr. Ackerman. Even some of Paul's white classmates acknowledged that "Baldy," as the students called him, was a "very prejudiced man." Ackerman disapproved when Paul was made glee club soloist, and he disliked the enthusiasm the other students showed for Paul during baseball or football games. His dislike was not lost on the boy, it seems, or his father. One day Ackerman sent Paul home as a punishment for tardiness. Paul was often late, though he lived just across the street from school. But when Reverend Robeson started to chastise him, Paul screamed at the old man: "Listen Pop, I'm bigger now. I don't care what you do to me, but if that hateful old principal ever lays a hand on me, I swear I'll try to break his neck."⁹ Although Reverend Robeson deeply believed that a "good boy" did not sass his teacher—he had given the teachers permission to paddle Paul if he misbehaved, and they had done that more than once—on this occasion he did not push the matter further.

Paul recalled disobeying his father only once—causing the old man to run after him, stumble, and knock out a tooth. Horrified and ashamed of himself, Paul remembered his "ingratitude" whenever he was tempted to disobey in the future—and usually did not.

During Paul's senior year in 1914-1915 the Robesons learned of competitive examinations, open to New Jersey residents, for a four-year scholarship to Rutgers. Although the Robesons had always assumed that Paul would go to Lincoln, Reverend Robeson's financial load was heavy and a scholarship for Paul would be a godsend. His chances to win didn't look good, however. Although Paul was at the top of his class, no one at Somerville had informed him of the examinations. He had therefore missed the preliminary qualifying examinations, covering earlier high school work, held the previous spring. He would have to be examined for all four high school years in the same three hours in which others would be tested only on their senior work.

Paul studied intensively. When Ben, Marion, or Bill were home from school, they drilled him; and his classmates and teachers, with the exception of "Baldy" Ackerman, cheered him on. But the greatest encouragement was the quiet confidence of his father, who was often at his side, as night after night he pored over the books. It was encouragement that paid off. Paul got the highest score on the examination that year and won not only the coveted scholarship but a belief in himself that would steady him all of his life. "Deep in my heart from that day on," he wrote forty years later, "was a conviction which none of the Ackermans of America would ever be able to shake. Equality might be denied, but I *knew* I was not inferior."[10]

Studying didn't stop his extracurricular activities. In the spring Paul took part in a statewide oratorical contest. Prodded by his brother Bill, he chose a speech with strong political overtones, though he was less concerned with the viewpoint than with applying English teacher Anna Miller's lessons in forensics and diction. He recited Wendell Phillips's speech on Toussaint L'Ouverture, the great Haitian general, which was particularly timely, since President Woodrow Wilson had just ordered the occupation of Haiti by the Marines. Toussaint L'Ouverture, Dessalines, King Christophe of Haiti were proud black names that symbolized a dream of freedom. So American blacks loudly protested the violation of Haiti's sovereignty, and the killing of several hundred Haitians in the invasion angered and outraged them. Before a predominantly white audience Paul quoted L'Ouverture's attack on white supremacy. "God gave us liberty; France has no right to take it away. Burn the cities, destroy the harvests, tear up the roads with cannon, poison the wells, show the white man the hell he comes to make." Not surprisingly, he lost the contest to a black youth from Asbury Park, New Jersey, who won first place, and a white girl who won second.

That same eventful spring another incident occurred that made Paul realize how exceptional his acceptance by the whites at Somerville High School was. His class, the class of 1915, was to be the first to make a trip to Washington, D.C. He excitedly joined his classmates in putting on plays and selling chocolate to get enough money for a private railroad car, until the Metropolitan Hotel in Washington informed the class it would not be accommodated if a black pupil was with them. The trip was not canceled, though some in the class protested. Instead, Paul, who was to graduate in June with the highest marks in the history of Somerville High, stayed behind.

That summer, he went to Narragansett, Rhode Island, a favorite spot for vacation employment for blacks. When Paul was fourteen his brother Ben had gotten him a job as kitchen boy at the resort, scrubbing stacks of pots and pans, peeling potatoes, fetching items for the chefs, cooks, and helpers. This time he worked as a waiter alongside his brother. One of the first people Ben introduced him to was Fritz Pollard of Brown University, the only black playing varsity football for an Ivy League college. Paul and Fritz, who was also working as a waiter, easily became friends. In a few months they would meet on opposing teams.

"Robeson of Rutgers"

II:

All-American

In the century and a half of its existence Rutgers had had only two black students. The realization that he would be its third and, for four years, probably its sole black, was undoubtedly a lonely and bewildering prospect for Paul when he arrived on campus in the fall of 1915. Somerville High had not been completely free of racial incidents; but there had been a few other black students, and, of course, he had lived at home. Now, for the first time, he would be away from his father. Denied dormitory space because he was black, he roomed with a black family on Murrell Street in New Brunswick.

Robeson's reputation as an athlete had preceded him to Rutgers. Football coach George Foster Sanford, who kept an eye on promising high school teams, had been impressed by his performance for Somerville High. Sanford had coached at Yale and been head coach at Columbia; he knew that there were few blacks on varsity teams. Brown had Fritz Pollard, who had made headlines when that team beat Yale in 1914. But Rutgers had never had a black on its team, and Sanford, uncertain as to how Paul would be accepted, had refrained from inviting him to the late summer training camp at Red Bank for varsity and promising freshmen. Nevertheless, when Paul got to Rutgers, he wanted to play. "Rutgers had a great team that year," he recalled years later. Brushing aside his worries Coach Sanford decided to try Robeson out; he sent him to the scrub team.

When the varsity saw Paul come on the field with the other scrubs, they decided to make it clear that he was not wanted in the Rutgers eleven. It was the first day of practice, and they might as well settle it right away. The scrimmage had hardly begun when one first-stringer knocked Paul down with a punch that broke his nose. Another player kneed him as he lay flat on his back. When it was all over, he had a broken nose, a dislocated shoulder, and "plenty of cuts and bruises." As a result of the battering, he would have to spend days in bed.

As Robeson recalled later, he often thought of quitting while he was recuperating. But then he remembered how his father had stressed that wherever he was and whatever he did he represented a lot of boys who did not have his opportunity. His brother Ben, who paid a visit, said to him, "If you want to quit school go ahead, but I wouldn't like to think and our father wouldn't like to think that our family had a quitter in it." Paul stayed, and about ten days later he was back on the field.

The varsity players were still out to get him. In one scrimmage Paul was on the ground just after making a tackle. Suddenly, a first-stringer came out of nowhere and stepped down hard on Paul's right hand. When he dragged his cleats away, all of Paul's fingernails went with them. But with his hand bandaged, Paul told the scrubs gathered around him that he was not quitting. Many years later he described what happened in the next play. "The whole first-string backfield came at me. I swept out my arms . . . and then three men running interference went down. The ball carrier was a first-class back named Kelly. I wanted to kill him, and I meant to kill him. It wasn't a thought, it was just a feeling. I got Kelly in my two hands and I heaved him up over my head." Just as Paul was about to dash the ball carrier to the ground, he heard Coach Sanford yell, "Robey, you're on the varsity."[1]

Almost from that moment he became a legend in Rutgers football history. But it was not only as a brillant football player that the *Daily Targum*, the college paper, and newspapers all over the country recorded the exploits of "Robeson of Rutgers." He also excelled as a catcher for the school's baseball team, a center in basketball, and a javelin thrower in track. Yet social ostracizing dogged Paul's heels ceaselessly. He was not invited to join the Rutgers Glee Club because of the social events that followed their concerts.

Whenever his studies and athletic activities permitted, he went back to Somerville to see his father. In turn, the old man often came to see Paul on the football field and, abandoning his usual dignified air, cheered with the coeds when his beloved boy made a good play. Paul also used the frequent occasions when he was in Somerville to see old friends—the Moore brothers, Fred and Warren; Stanley Douglas, the brother of Winston who had been the only other Negro player on Robeson's high school football team. Winston was making a name for himself in athletics at Lincoln, and Paul often visited him there. Old friends from Princeton—Charlie Chew and Arthur and Willie

Moore—also attended Lincoln; and several of the girls from Somerville, Margaret Potter among them, attended Trenton Normal School, so some weekends and holidays were occasions for carefree partying.

When he was home, his father often reminded him that athletics were secondary to scholarship, though Paul hardly needed reminding. He was good at his studies. He helped his friend Malcolm Pitt with Greek, and in turn Pitt, who later became dean of the Kennedy School of Missions of Hartford Theological Seminary, helped him with trigonometry. Both devoted to academic achievement, Paul and Malcolm were close companions for the four years they were at Rutgers, only partly because the accident of their last names— beginning with "R" and "P"—threw them together from the first day of registration to commencement.

In April 1917 Congress declared war against the Central Powers. Black Americans were among the first to volunteer, and more than 200,000 served overseas, all in segregated units. They went enthusiastically, hopeful that in making the "world safe for democracy," in their President's phrase, they would help make democracy a reality at home. Ben Robeson enlisted and was named Chaplain of the Fifteenth Regiment of New York State.

This must have been on Paul's mind when, during his junior year, he took note of black participation in every national conflict beginning with the Revolutionary War. In a speech entitled "Loyalty and the American Negro," he outlined the role black Americans played in these wars and won first prize in third-year extemporaneous speaking. Paul's speeches were generally stirring, having been often rehearsed before his father. Paul admired the old man's delivery, which was in the tradition of the old-time black preacher, and he tried to emulate the voice that could range from a gong-like clap of thunder to an ear-straining whisper.

That fall, when Rutgers met the mighty Naval Reserve team, composed of all-stars from football powerhouses across the nation, the *New York Tribune* wrote:

> *A tall, tapering Negro in a faded crimson sweater, moleskins and a pair of maroon socks ranged hither and yon on a wind-whipped Flatbush field yesterday afternoon. He rode on the wings of the frigid breezes; a grim, silent, and compelling figure. . . The Negro was PR of Rutgers College, and he is a minister's son. He is also nineteen years of age and weighs two hundred pounds. Of his*

football capacity you are duly referred to Cupid Black of Newport and Yale. He can tell you. It was Robeson, a veritable Othello of battle, who led the dashing little Rutgers eleven to a 14-0 victory over the widely heralded Newport Naval Reserves . . .

In Robeson's junior year, Walter Camp, the dean of football, named him to the All-American football team as an end, calling him "the greatest defensive back ever to trod the gridiron." He was the first All-American Rutgers had ever produced in any sport, yet Paul's contributions to the team—which included excellent play as pass receiver, end, and defense—didn't spare him from agonizing bias. When Rutgers was to play Washington and Lee, a Virginia college, officials and students there objected to playing against a black man, and Coach Sanford decided to withdraw Paul from the starting lineup rather than to cancel the game. Paul was deeply humiliated, and he must have felt some satisfaction when Rutgers had to settle for a 13-13 tie. During the same season after a game against Syracuse, a Syracuse student named Samuel Rosen, who had been impressed by the way Paul "dominated the proceedings" waited out on the street "to get a look at him." The Rutgers squad emerged gregarious in their victory, but Paul was not among them. Finally, Paul came out—tall, proud, and all alone. "It was my first insight into a pain, and pride and a struggle which in one form or another continued throughout his life . . . From that moment (Paul) began teaching me that struggle is a fact of life."[2] They eventually became close friends.

In May Paul was summoned back to Somerville, to his father's sickbed. He had known the old man was not well, and indeed had occasionally filled in for his father in the pulpit, but it was much more serious than he realized. William Drew Robeson died on May 17 at the age of seventy-three years. The Somerville newspaper eulogized him as "a man of strong character (who) quickly resented any attempt to belittle [his race] or to interfere with their rights." Nearly sixty years later his name is still mentioned in Princeton and Somerville with reverence.

Paul was profoundly shaken by his father's death. He would no longer be able to lean on his father's rock-like strength, gentle love, and abiding concern, but he vowed not to become paralyzed with grief. As if he were building a monument to his father, Paul put in longer and longer hours of study, feeling that "Pop," as he called him, was with him as he pored over Virgil and Homer. At the end of his junior year, only a few weeks after Reverend Robeson's death, Paul won his Phi Beta Kappa key, a real distinction for a third-year student.

Now that his father was gone, Paul's need for money to supplement his scholarship was even greater. So he went back to work at Narrangansett that summer. One day a hotel guest, tired of hearing the friendly black headwaiter boast, "That waiter there is Paul Robeson of Rutgers, All-American end," began criticizing and insulting Paul. He complained of his service and insisted upon the waiter's being "a servant, not an All-American." Paul felt his anger rising. He knew if he stayed he would do something he would regret. So he left the dining room, took off his jacket, and went to the waiters' quarters, where he sat for hours without speaking. For days he stayed in his quarters, or played football with the other waiters, until the offensive guest left.[3]

Paul's senior year at Rutgers was marked by new athletic achievements. Once again, Walter Camp named him All-American end, in 1918. In a javelin-throwing contest he hurled the spear more than 137 feet against a strong wind to beat his nearest competitor by a dozen feet. He played catcher on the baseball team, and in his final baseball game helped pull his team to a 5-1 win over Princeton. It was an especially sweet victory, since Rutgers had not beaten its rival in an athletic contest since the first football game ever held in America, between Rutgers and Princeton, had been played a half-century earlier. All these feats earned him letters in four different sports that last year at Rutgers, for a total of fifteen, and undoubtedly helped, with his academic record, elect him to Cap and Skull, the exclusive senior fraternity made up of four men "who most truly and fully represented the finest ideals and traditions of Rutgers."

Paul also continued his debating, and one publication called him "an orator of exceptional ability." He won almost every elocution contest he entered, and when, as a senior, he spoke on "The War's Effect on American Manhood," he won the Ann Van Nest Bussing Prize in Extempore Speaking. It seemed natural then that Paul should deliver the commencement oration when he graduated in June 1919, more natural still that he should speak on "Interracial Relations."

The Class Prophecy predicted that Paul would become the governor of New Jersey, a considerable irony, given the general disenfranchisement of the Negro in 1919. A more telling indication of how he was generally perceived by his fellows was the *Targum's* final appraisal of his college career: "He has dimmed the fame of Booker T. Washington and is the leader of the colored race in America." Gushy collegiate chatter. But it provides a clue to Robeson's character in those closing Rutgers days. Obviously he was among Du Bois's Talented Tenth;

indeed he would have been among the talented tenth of the nation, white or black, had the nation been willing to recognize it. He believed in conciliation, in integration. He endorsed closer cooperation between the races, if whites could help blacks secure their rights. He rejected no offers of white help, if in accepting he did not compromise his goals. He affirmed these goals before leaving New Brunswick in a speech to the town's leading citizens who had honored him at a banquet. "I want my life work to be a memorial to my father's training and to be not for my own self but to help my people to a higher life."[4]

Reverend Robeson had hoped Paul would become a minister, and indeed, Paul had never lost contact with his father's congregation. "He used to come back and sing for us at the church concerts," one of the members of that church recalled. On these occasions he would intersperse the songs with sermons and bits of philosophy. "He was always the same Paul every time you met him," the parishioner continued. "Learnin' didn't go to his head." Still, Paul felt he was too fun-loving, "not good enough" for what he thought a minister ought to be. No, he was convinced that the best way to "help my people" was to study law. Accepted at both Harvard and Columbia law schools, he chose Columbia, because he wanted to live in Harlem.

His choice of law as a career was a reflection of his still unshaken belief in the ideals of American democracy and the promise of the American dream. In his senior thesis, "The Fourteenth Amendment, the Sleeping Giant of the American Constitution," he had interpreted the due process and equal protection clause, concluding: "Of all the forces that have acted in strengthening the bonds of our Union, in protecting our civil rights from invasion, in assuring the perpetuity of our institutions and making us truly a nation, the Fourteenth Amendment is the greatest . . . This Amendment is a vital part of American Constitutional Law and we hardly know its sphere, but its provisions must be duly observed and conscientiously interpreted so that through it . . . the American people shall develop a higher sense of Constitutional morality."

Across the paper, his professor penciled, *Extravagant*.

III:
Home to Harlem

In the summer of Paul's graduation from Rutgers, America was swept by a wave of violence. It was 1919, the "Red Summer," the greatest period of antiblack riots the country had ever known. Beginning in June there were twenty-five outbreaks in which whites, often egged on by a revived Ku Klux Klan, burned homes, attacked blacks on the streets, and dragged them from streetcars. Special targets of their rampages were discharged black soldiers who had been "spoiled" by France's racial openness. Some of them were lynched while still in uniform.

Much of this violence, aimed at keeping blacks from "stepping out of their place," was based on attitudes that had been formed during the first two decades of the twentieth century. Jim Crow had taken over, dashing the hope of blacks that Theodore Roosevelt's election as President would usher in a new era. Roosevelt had favored restrictions on voting rights, defended lynching for alleged violations against white women, and advised blacks not to seek to enter the professions. Roosevelt's successor, President Taft, in an address to students at Biddle University, the black institution that Paul's brother Ben had attended, declared that the race problem could only be solved by sending blacks out of the country. He told his audience, "Your race is adapted to be a race of farmers, first, last, and for all times." Woodrow Wilson, shortly after he became the first southern president since the Civil War, wrote his old college acquaintance Thomas Dixon, author of such antiblack novels as *The Leopard's Spots* and *The Clansman:* "We are handling . . . the colored people . . . in the departments in just the way they ought to be handled. We are trying and by degrees succeeding in a plan. . . ."[1] The plan, which he carried out, was to reverse a fifty-year-old policy and segregate federal agencies in Washington. In government offices, partitions were erected between black and white workers. Hotels, restaurants, and theaters in Washington followed suit.

Any doubts that the President's attitudes were shared by millions of other Americans were dispelled by the enormous popularity of D.W. Griffith's film, *The Birth of a Nation* (based on *The Clansman*), which presents blacks as a menace to society unless checked by the Ku Klux Klan. In 1915, the first year of its run, an estimated 5 million or more, about 6 percent of the population flocked to see the film. When it was shown at the White House, President Wilson is reported to have said, "It is like writing history in lightning. My only regret is that it is all so terribly true."[2] Members of the Supreme Court and Congress also were shown the film, and the Ku Klux Klan, which had been revived in Georgia in 1915, even used it in recruiting members. In the South advertisements for *Birth of a Nation* often carried the happy news, "It will make you hate."

Brutality against blacks continued in the last five years of the second decade. In 1916 a black man was buried alive in Waco, Texas, before a cheering mob of men, women, and children, and a well-to-do black farmer was lynched for refusing the price offered for his cottonseed. The next year, forty blacks were killed in a riot in East St. Louis, Illinois.

America's entry into World War I in 1917 gave blacks hope that the tide of hatred and violence against them would turn. Many blacks migrated to the North, where they found better job opportunities and living conditions because of the wartime economy. Black soldiers serving overseas did not fail to notice that they were treated more equally by foreigners than by their fellow Americans. By April 1919 some black troops had begun to return, many of them resolved to struggle for the same treatment at home. In May the editor of *The Crisis*, wrote in their name, "We return from slavery of uniform which the world's madness demanded us to don to the freedom of civil garb. We stand again to look America squarely in the face and call a spade a spade. We sing: This country of ours, despite all its better souls have done and dreamed, is yet a shameful land." The nation's response was the "Red Summer."

At the end of this season of strife, Paul was invited to speak about social problems to a group at the New Brunswick YMCA. "The Future of the Negro in America and What Shall His Place Be in American Life" was the title of his talk. Comparison of the progress of blacks with that of whites over the past fifty years was unjust, he said. Not only did the black "have to concede a head start of centuries to the white, but he was also forced to progress under great difficulties."[3] He spoke of inadequate educational facilities and unjust treatment and pointed out that blacks, in spite of tremendous handicaps, had shown their willingness to serve America dutifully in both the Civil War and the Great War. His solution to the racial problem was closer cooperation, "both working for the good of both."

Twenty-one-years-old, Paul now was 6'2" tall and weighed 215 pounds. His body was taut, and he walked with a curious gait— alternately ambling uncertainly or striding purposefully. In the fashion of the time he wore his thick hair cropped close. His emotions were easily reflected in his face: In somber moments the lower lip of the wide mouth tended to set in a pout; when he laughed, the nostrils of his broad, strong nose flared wide. He jaw was clean-shaven and firmly set, and the muscles of his face sometimes quivered when he was angry or upset. He was not exactly handsome. But with his cappucino complexion, his dark eyes that stared straight at you with determination and a sort of confused nobility, his booming voice, and his magnificent physique, he was already a presence.

Harlem was entering its heyday when Paul first arrived in the final months of 1919. World War I was over, and America sighed with relief as it prepared to go on what F. Scott Fitzgerald described as "the greatest, gaudiest spree in its history." With loose cash and looser morals crowds of whites in search of new forms of entertainment made their way up to 125th Street to gape at "Negro life" and listen to jazz, while they drank illegal whiskey. The Cotton Club and Small's Paradise dominated Seventh Avenue; and Jungle Alley overflowed with restaurants, bars, and clubs, many of them owned by whites and closed to blacks. One of these clubs even refused to admit W.C. Handy, composer of the "St. Louis Blues," to hear his own music. This was the white tourist Harlem.

For blacks Harlem was much more than a playground. It was home for the hardworking people who were the bulk of its population and who never saw the inside of the Cotton Club or Connie's, as well as for the six or seven millionaires and the middle-class people who lived on "Striver's Row" and Sugar Hill. For blacks across America and even abroad it was the symbol of a new era, the era of the "new Negro," the age of the "Black Renaissance."

The spirit of the Negro Renaissance, like the spirit of the 1920s, was embodied, as Nathan Huggins puts it in *Harlem Renaissance*, in "words of emancipation, innovation, and newness." But the black intellectuals who decried economic and social injustices in a rush of poetry, fiction, drama, and music, were not political revolutionaries. As John Hope Franklin remarks, they were not rebelling, "they were protesting against the inefficient operation of the system."[4] The center of activity for this new breed was Harlem. It was the home of the writer, poet, and former U.S. Consul to Venezuela and Nicaragua, James Weldon Johnson, who with his brother J. Rosamond Johnson and Bob Cole had successfully written songs and plays for the New York musical stage. His *Book of American Negro Poetry*, published in 1922, included the works of outstanding contemporary black poets, like Claude McKay, whose "Harlem Shadows" also appeared in 1922 and whose "If We Must Die" and "To the White Friends," seemed to many to epitomize with their proud defiance and biting contempt the "reawakening" in process. McKay lived in Harlem, as did Jean Toomer, whose realistic stories about blacks were published under the title *Cane* in 1923, and Langston Hughes, the rebel poet, who expressed the new mood of determination not only to overcome the Jim Crow system, but "to express our individual dark-skinned selves without fear or shame." And, of course, there was New York-born Countee Cullen, who in a few years would mark a new high in the Negro Renaissance with the publication of *Color*, his first volume of poems.

The forerunner of all these men was another Harlem resident, W. E. B. Du Bois, who had written artistic works of protest for nearly a quarter-century. In February 1919 he had dramatically called a Pan-African conference in Paris to plead the cause of darker peoples before the world. Fifty-seven delegates attended, including sixteen American Negroes, twenty West Indians, and twelve Africans. As editor of *The Crisis*, the magazine of the National Association for the Advancement of Colored People, he waged a continuous campaign against lynching and mob rule. His books and articles were important cultural milestones.

Another Harlem resident who, like Du Bois, was important in putting black social thought onto the international scene was the Jamaican Marcus Garvey, leader of the Universal Negro Improvement Association. For nearly a decade the flamboyant and charismatic Garvey was the idol of countless common men in the United States, Latin America, the Caribbean, and Africa with his appeals to black race pride and dreams of restoring Africa to the Africans, much to the disdain of intellectuals like Du Bois.

With Harlem as the center of the black universe, it was little wonder that Paul called it his "homeground." In the beginning its well-known residents were merely names to the twenty-year-old Rutgers graduate, but he thrilled to the vitality he found on almost every street corner. Walking down 137th Street or Lenox Avenue, he found that his exploits as a football player had made him something of a celebrity to people of all walks of life. And he responded to their admiring glances and greetings with his warmth and booming laughter.

Paul entered Columbia University Law School in February 1920. "There were six blacks in my class, Paul Robeson being the most memorable," wrote Supreme Court Justice William O. Douglas in his memoirs.[5] "He was very sociable," the Justice recalled in an interview a half-century later.[6] "He wasn't on the law review"; he was deep into his music." Among his other classmates were athletes with and against whom he had played during his years at Rutgers, as well as boys from Somerville. But Paul didn't have much time to socialize. In addition to his studies he had to work to pay his fees, feed, and clothe himself. Through Fritz Pollard, whom he met in Harlem, Paul took a job briefly as assistant football coach at Lincoln, where Pollard was head coach. He took advantage of his presence on that all-black campus to join Alpha Phi Alpha fraternity, "the oldest Negro college fraternity." Using his voice to earn money for law school, Paul sang with "The Four Harmony Kings," which included jazz bandleader Fletcher Henderson, in the fabulous *Shuffle Along,* and at the Cotton Club in a show with the diminutive and dynamic Florence Mills. Another job during law school was playing professional football with the Akron Indians and later the Milwaukee Badgers, on weekends. Occasionally, during his rare moments of leisure, he would drop by Harlem's Lafayette Theater to catch the plays by the stock company, particularly enjoying sensuous Abbie Mitchell and an intense actor named Charles Gilpin.

Early in 1921 Paul met Eslanda Cardozo Goode. She was a graduate student in chemistry at Columbia University, a daughter of the small black upper class of educated professionals and businessmen. "Gentle Negroes," she called them then. Caramel-colored, with sparkling brown eyes, an attractive presence, and a dynamic personality, Essie Goode was a descendant of the black branch of the South Carolina Cardozos, whose Jewish branch had produced U.S. Supreme Court Justice Benjamin Cardozo. Francis Lewis Cardozo, Essie's maternal grandfather, was born free in Charleston in 1837 and educated in South Carolina, at the University of Glasgow, and the Presbyterian theological seminaries in Edinburgh and London. In 1865 Cardozo was pastor of the Temple Congregational Church in New Haven, and at the end of the Civil War he returned to South Carolina, where he founded Avery Institute, a normal school. He was elected to the state constitutional convention in 1868, and he eventually became secretary of state and treasurer of South Carolina. During this time he studied law at the University of South Carolina, graduating in 1876. A year later Cardozo moved to Washington, where he taught Latin at Howard University and worked in the Post Office Department. For nineteen years he was a principal in the Colored Public Schools System, and in 1928 a business high school was named for him. Essie's father, Frank Goode, was estranged from her mother, Eslanda Cardozo Goode, and though she was born in Washington, in 1896, she grew up with her mother and two brothers in New York. Mrs. Goode worked as a masseuse to send Essie through college, first to the University of Chicago, where she majored in chemistry, and later to Columbia University for her graduate degree. "She was very advanced mentally over all of us," her cousin, Mrs. Elizabeth Barker of Washington, D.C., remembered.

Paul's tall frame, towering over the five-foot Essie, soon became a familiar sight at the doctor's house on 139th Street where Essie rented a room. While calling on Essie he got to know two other lodgers, her friend Minnie Sumner, a seamstress, and a young lawyer named William Patterson, whom Langston Hughes would later describe as "brilliant but dogmatic." Patterson, recalling those days, said that Paul was drawn by Essie's intellectuality. "I think he saw she would be very helpful (in handling the harsher side of the city) for she was very aggressive." And, as Essie said, "There was no trace of aggressiveness in (Paul's) make-up." For her part, Essie was impressed with Paul's "masculinity (and) the fact that it was clear that he was an extraordinary figure—a man of . . . intelligence and talent."[7]

Since Paul considered Princeton home, it was a measure of his seriousness about Essie that he took her there on Memorial Day 1921 to meet his relatives and friends. The holiday was a traditional fun day for black Princetonians—who called themselves "Black Princes" in considerable irony. The custom of the day was to gorge on potato salad, fried chicken, and greens and polish it all off with rhubarb wine. This occasion was memorable, however, because the wine hadn't finished brewing and three of the Princes landed in the hospital.

After a six-month courtship Paul and Essie announced their engagement at a brilliant party in Chicago, reported in vivid detail in the *Chicago Defender*. They were married among friends and kin on August 17, 1921 in Rye, New York.

By now Essie was working as an analytical chemist in the Surgical Pathology Department at Presbyterian Hospital of the Columbia Medical Center, having been recommended for the position by one of her professors. She was the first black person ever to hold the job. Meanwhile, as Paul returned to his studies, Essie was reacting to the stir of creative activity generated by the Harlem Renaissance. Paul had a "gorgeous bass voice"[8] and dramatic flair, and Essie wondered whether these gifts might be used somehow in the theater. She felt that dramatics might offer him some outlet for his strong emotions. At any rate, when she heard that the Harlem YMCA was reviving *Simon the Cyrenian,* one of three one-act plays written by Ridgely Torrence under the title of *Granny Maumee,* she insisted that Paul take the role of Simon. Paul was not very interested, but Essie was so persistent that he agreed to take the part.

Essie did not stop there. So convinced was she of her husband's talents, that she invited Kenneth Macgowan and Robert Edmond Jones of the Provincetown Playhouse in Greenwich Village to come up to the Harlem "Y" and see Robeson act. As became obvious later, they were impressed, but for the time being, no reviews appeared, and Paul did not take the acting incident very seriously. He went home, forgot about the theater, and returned to law school the next morning as if nothing had happened.

Other influential theater people had seen the play, nevertheless. When Augustin Duncan, brother of dancer Isadora Duncan, was preparing a production of *Taboo,* by Mary Hoyt Wiborg, he remembered Paul's performance and cast him opposite the English actress Margaret Wycherly. It was a loosely constructed and rather bad play, which opened on a southern plantation and flashed back to Africa, but that didn't matter to Paul, who needed the money; in addition to his speaking role he sang several songs. "I knew little of what I was doing, but I was urged to go ahead and try," explained Paul.[9] Evidently he succeeded, for except for a blistering critique by Alexander Woollcott, the reviews were generally favorable to Paul. It was no surprise, then, that he was asked to join the cast that summer when they toured the English provinces with the same play, under the new title *Voodoo.* This time Mrs. Patrick Campbell starred in it, supported by the original black cast from New York.

Paul's first trip to England, beginning with rehearsals in London, was unforgettable. The absence of the Jim Crow laws that ruled America seemed to cleanse his soul and underscore the sense of equality he had always felt but that he had been unable to fully express. "The contrast," he said, was "wonderful."[10] Later visits would alter that view, but for the time being it was an exhilarating experience for the twenty-four-year-old law student. Robeson was staying at the flat of a black singer named John Payne, along with a third black American—twenty-nine-year-old pianist Lawrence Brown. Brown, who had grown up in Florida, was in England partly as an accompanist for singer Roland Hayes, but he spent his spare time arranging and scoring spirituals, some of which had never been recorded. It was more than just a hobby for the devoted musician, who had been inspired, while still in America, by Ernest Bloch's settings of the 114th and 137th Psalms and the composer's stated intention "to express the soul of the Jewish people." Brown had resolved to try to do the same for blacks.

One evening, for fun, the exuberant Robeson sang some spirituals. Brown was deeply impressed with the "magnificent natural voice" of the tall New Yorker and, sure that Paul could become a great singer, later sent him the volume of spirituals he had scored.

The tour of the English provinces and Scotland in *Voodoo* was a great success. In Edinburgh a critic commented, "There is nothing more striking than the part played by the big Negro whose simplicity is sound art." Mrs. Campbell was so impressed with her young supporting actor that she wanted him to play Othello. But Paul was not to be deterred from law school. Theater and concerts were "farthest from my mind, this trip was just a lark. Instead of waiting tables in hotels to earn money, I was being paid 20 pounds or so a week for expenses to walk on stage. Say a few lines—sing a song or two. Just too good for words."[11]

In the fall of 1922 he returned to Columbia for his final term. Faced with the ever-pressing problem of money for tuition, food, housing, and clothing—although his summer work in England had helped and Essie was still at the clinic laboratory—he continued to play professional football on weekends. He had never been particularly pleased with this method of earning money, but a fight that occurred as the result of a game turned him against it permanently. One day the team he was playing on trounced that of the legendary Jim Thorpe, the American Indian who had been an American decathlon winner in the early 1900s, so soundly that Thorpe approached Robeson after the game with a threatening look in his eye. Robeson's team vanished, leaving him to defend himself alone against Thorpe's entire squad. He protected himself so well that two Chicago fight promoters offered to train him to challenge Jack Dempsey, then the world's heavyweight champion. Perhaps they thought that Robeson would at least conduct himself more to their liking than the death-defying, danger-loving Jack Johnson, with his flamboyant lifestyle and well-known preference for white women. The promoters apparently floated a rumor that Paul was going to box professionally because he could not make ends meet practicing law, but when they showed up on Robeson's doorstep in Harlem, he threw them out in a rage. Boxing was connected with the semi-underworld, he said, and he would have nothing to do with it. Yet the rumor persisted. In early 1923 George Daly, writing in the *World,* called it "a printed fantasy," which so upset Paul that he fired off a letter branding the rumors "absolutely untrue and unfounded." Looking back on the episode from the perspective of two decades, Paul said, "I would have done anything rather than that! Anything!"[12]

Paul graduated from Columbia in February 1923. He was offered a political job to tide him over until he could build up his practice, but he rejected it "because of the many enforced allegiances it entailed." He read law occasionally with his classmates and friends but "did not bestir himself to find a job." By Essie's accounts: "He was not the person to think out what he would do or wanted to do and then go out and try and do it. . . . He idled away month after month, waiting for something that would interest him to come along. One by one the fellows in his class found posts, but not Paul. He often dropped into offices to see them, to talk over cases with them, but that was all."[13]

Getting a job commensurate with one's education and ability was extremely difficult for a black man, even one of Robeson's renown. The American Bar Association excluded blacks from membership, and work for black lawyers was severely limited to politically uninfluential areas or relegated to organizations within the black community. Paul could have given his energy and talents to black organizations, such as the fledgling NAACP, but he avoided this route. In those days, he seemed to believe that genuine success in any venture meant entrance into the white world.

After several months of inactivity, he found a job writing briefs for a downtown law firm. One brief that he drew up on a phase of the famous *Gould Will* case was so well prepared that it was used by the firm when the case was brought to trial. Paul enjoyed the work, but eventually the clerks and other members of the firm objected to his presence in the office. When, after a couple of weeks, a secretary refused to take dictation from him, Paul put on his hat, walked out, and never returned.

He returned to Harlem and tried to plan his next step. "I'll wait a little," he said, "something will turn up." This attitude frankly disturbed Essie, who expected a more consistent drive to succeed, but eventually she came to understand that what at first looked "almost like pathological laziness" in her husband was really "a remarkable discretion," a guiding instinct.[14] For his part Paul called it "a core which stopped me from being shattered during difficult times."[15] And indeed the times were difficult as he waited month after month in late 1923 and early 1924 for "something to turn up." What turned up was an invitation for him to star in another play.

IV:
Enter
Eugene O'Neill

In February 1924 readers of New York newspapers learned that Paul Robeson, "a full-blooded Negro," and an unidentified white actress would be cast as man and wife in a Provincetown Playhouse production of Eugene O'Neill's *All God's Chillun Got Wings*. What at first might have appeared to be a mere theater item proved, in the months that followed, to be much more. Four years before, the Provincetown Players had staged O'Neill's *The Emperor Jones* with black actor Charles Gilpin in the role of Brutus. Until that time it had been the rule in the American theater and cinema for important black roles to be played by whites, and even some Provincetowners, whose work was considered avant-garde, had argued that the public would only accept a white man in blackface as the ex-Pullman porter from Harlem. Others thought the role should be played by a black, and they eventually won out. *The Emperor Jones* opened on November 1, 1920, to immediate success. Gilpin, widely praised, continued in the role during the play's 204 performances and two seasons on the road. The year after his opening the New York Drama League named him one of the ten people who had contributed most to the 1920-1921 season; ironically, however, he could not be invited to its annual dinner, since some of the league's members objected to dining with a black. Only after a protest by Eugene O'Neill and many of the others who were to be honored, including David Belasco, and a threat by many of the actors to decline their own invitations, did the league finally give in.

Despite Gilpin's acclaim, his relations with O'Neill had become irreparably strained by the time the Provincetown Playhouse decided on a revival of *The Emperor Jones*. Gilpin had disliked the frequent use of the word "nigger" in the scripts, and when he substituted "Negro" or "colored man" and made other changes, O'Neill had become furious and threatened to fire him. And there were other nagging questions for the actor. Not long after the opening of *Jones*, he said, "If I were white a dozen opportunities would come to me as a result of a success like this. But I'm black. It is no joke when I ask myself, 'Where do I go from here?' It has been demonstrated that a play can be written that will give a colored actor a chance. Perhaps someone will write another such play." For relief from these problems, Gilpin began drinking, not only offstage, but at times both before and during a performance.

Obviously a replacement for Gilpin would be necessary for the revival. When it came to casting the part, Kenneth Macgowan and Robert Edmond Jones remembered the young black they had seen at the Harlem YMCA. O'Neill responded enthusiastically: "I've corralled a young fellow with considerable experience, wonderful presence and voice, full of ambition and a damn fine man personally with real brains—not a 'ham.' This guy deserves his chance and I don't believe he'll lose his head if he makes a hit—as he surely will, for he's read the play for me and I'm sure he'll be bigger than Gilpin was even at the start,"[1] O'Neill wrote writer and editor Mike Gold in 1923. O'Neill had chosen Paul Robeson not only as Brutus in *The Emperor Jones*, but also as Jim Harris in the newly finished *All God's Chillun Got Wings*. Paul had agreed because he needed the money. "The 75 a week which they offered me was a good salary in those days and I accepted."[2]

The new play was about a young black, Jim Harris, and a white girl, Ella Downey, who grow up in a poor, racially mixed neighborhood and eventually marry. Jim, who is studying for the bar examination, is beset with self-doubt and prejudice and places his wife on a pedestal; Ella considers herself an outcast because of the marriage, but she is totally dependent on Jim and afraid that if Jim succeeds in passing the bar it will prove his superiority. She goes insane, making it impossible for Jim to study, and he fails the exam. Ella is ecstatic. In the final scene, as he admits defeat and resigns himself to taking care of her, she stoops in front of him and kisses his hand.

That closing gesture was only a small incident in the drama, but a New York-based news syndicate stirred up a national controversy when it sent out pre-opening-night pictures of Mary Blair captioned, "White Actress to Kiss Negro's Hand." The play's literary merit was forgotten as racist protests, aiming to prevent what playwright Augustus Thomas haughtily described as an "unnecessary concession to realism," were fired off to newspapers, the Provincetown Playhouse, and to New York City officials.

William Randolph Hearst's *American* led the opposition and reported rumors that two backers of the Greenwich Village theater were withdrawing their support in outrage and that the kissing scene had prompted countless blacks to subscribe to the theater. Both rumors proved to be false. Otto H. Kahn, the stockbroker, and art patroness Mrs. Willard Straight actually increased their support of the theater, and many Negroes attacked the play. The Reverend Adam Clayton Powell, Sr., disliked its intimation that blacks "are desirous of marrying white women."

Throughout rehearsals the *American* raised the specter of race riots if the play was staged and continued to publish protests from well-known groups and individuals. Some felt the play would "stir up racial antagonism" and took a stand against mixed casts; others found it in bad taste. The president of the Society for the Prevention of Crime said he hadn't read the play, but from what he had heard it was "a damnable thing to put on the stage." Hate letters poured in to the actors and to O'Neill in particular. The head of the Ku Klux Klan in Georgia threatened his son's life if the play opened. O'Neill sent the letter back with "Go Fuck Yourself" penciled in at the bottom.

O'Neill insisted that the play only portrayed "the special lives of individual human beings." In defense of the casting of Paul to play Jim Harris, he said, "I believe [Mr. Robeson] can portray the character better than any other actor, that's all there is to it . . ." The objections to Paul were, he felt, ridiculous. "Right in this city two years ago in a public theater he played opposite a distinguished white actress, Margaret Wycherly, in a play called *Voodoo*. In one of the scenes he was cast as the King and she the Queen. A King and Queen are, I believe, usually married."[3]

W. E. B. Du Bois came to O'Neill's defense, explaining that a black feared literary portrayal because his experiences had been distorted, sullied, and "seized by his enemies for . . . hateful propaganda . . . Eugene O'Neill is bursting (this shell). He has my sympathy, for his soul must be lame with the blows rained upon him. But it is work that must be done."[4]

Meanwhile, Paul was having problems of his own. Self-conscious about his size on the tiny stage, he frankly feared he could not act.

A publicity photo announcing Robeson as the protagonist of Eugene O'Neill's controversial *All God's Chillun Got Wings*

Robeson with co-star Mary Blair

Luckily, in the Provincetowners—James Light, who was to direct the production, O'Neill, Eleanor Fitzgerald, and Harold McGhee—he found the guidance and expert direction he so desperately needed. Light set about giving him confidence and helped him concentrate on the character and his emotions so that he could overcome the physical tensions created by his fear of the stage and of acting. He did not tell Robeson what to do nor show him how to do it. He did not tell him what to say. Rather, he simply sat quietly in the auditorium while Robeson felt his way. When Robeson came to a difficult speech, Light would go on stage, pull him down onto a small soapbox beside him, and then, thought by thought, word by word, together they would analyze the troublesome speech. Often O'Neill dropped by to help. As the rehearsals progressed, James Light, watching Robeson develop the character of Jim according to his own conception, had occasion more than once to feel that the actor "had a deeper feeling about his race than the theater could satisfy."

In March, Paul was asked to take on yet another part. *Rosanne*, a play about a sinful southern preacher whose congregation finally takes its revenge, had been enjoying a run in Philadelphia with Charles Gilpin in the leading role. A temporary replacement was needed for Gilpin, and Paul was chosen to play opposite Rose McClendon. But he did not let his performances in Philadelphia interfere with his New York rehearsals.

On May 6, a week before the scheduled opening of *Chillun*, the Provincetowners hastily revived *The Emperor Jones* with Robeson in this title role as well. Even with the added burden on Paul, it was a clever strategic move. The double bill that had been playing at the theater had failed to draw, and something was needed to bring in revenue until *Chillun* was ready. Besides, attention would be focused on Paul as an actor, rather than as a center of controversy. The role of Brutus Jones, an ex-Pullman porter who has set himself over the inhabitants of a West Indian island, "as yet not self-determined by White Marines," is a theatrical tour de force. He is the focus of action for five consecutive scenes as his subjects revolt against his tyranny and corruption and he attempts to escape through the jungle. There the maddening sound of drums and his own buried ghosts hound him, until he is stripped to his primitivism and captured and killed in the dawn.

Many of the first-nighters came, as the Provincetowners correctly predicted, because of the stir that was being raised over Robeson's role in the forthcoming *All God's Chillun*. Remembering Charles Gilpin's brilliant performance as Brutus Jones, they were cool to Paul at first.

But by the time the curtain fell, the audience exploded in a frenzy of applause, won over by Paul's amazing natural attributes, despite the sensitivity and strength of Gilpin's more polished performance. Charles Gilpin himself was present that night and somewhat uneasy about the young actor whom some were calling his equal. When James J. "Slim" Martin, a steelworker and part-time Provincetown player, asked him to join him in an after-theater drink, Gilpin said, "No, Slim, I feel kind of low. I created the role of the Emperor. That role belongs to me. That Irishman, he just wrote the play."[5] Many years later, O'Neill would come to agree, saying: "As I look back now on all my work, I can honestly say that there was only one actor who carried out every notion of a character I had in mind. That actor was Charles Gilpin. . . ."[6]

But for the time being the success was Paul's. His performance in *The Emperor Jones* received almost ecstatic reviews. Alexander Woollcott thought he was "brilliant"; Frank Vreeland wrote in the *Herald-Tribune* that Paul's portrayal of Brutus Jones was "as strong in its own right" as Gilpin's. The *New York Telegram and Evening Mail* described the audience's reaction to the young actor: "Robeson was dragged before the curtain by men and women who rose to their feet and applauded," it reported the next morning. "When the ache in their arms stopped their hands, they used their voices, shouted meaningless words, gave hoarse throaty cries . . . the ovation was for Robeson, for his emotional strength, for his superb acting."

Even the Negro press, which was reserved about the drama, thought Paul possessed the qualities that could make him transcend race as an actor. "Oh!" said the *Pittsburgh Courier*, "what a Brutus or Antony he would make."

After several delays *All God's Chillun Got Wings* was finally scheduled to open on May 15, though there were still some problems to confront. Riots had been widely predicted at the opening, and official harassment made the Provincetowners afraid to depend only on the city police on duty outside the Playhouse. They enlisted the help of "Slim" Martin, who hired one of his steelworker friends, "Slim" Nugent, to stand guard outside Paul's and Mary Blair's dressing rooms. Nugent was a tough ex-pug, but when he first saw Paul, he said to Martin, "Is that the big ape I'm supposed to guard? Well, listen, if anything starts, you and me just get out of his way and pile up the ones he knocks down." Other burly steelworkers were hired to stand at both ends of Macdougal Street.

Then, only hours before curtain time, the theater was denied permission for the eight black and white children called for in the script to appear in the early scenes. The Provincetowners considered postponing the opening night until midgets could be found to replace the children. But in the end they decided the best solution was to have Jimmy Light explain the problem to the audience and read the children's parts himself. (A few days later Mayor "Red Mike" Hylan's office said the rejection was based on the "tender age" of the children, who ranged in age from eleven to seventeen. That same week, however, a play opened on Broadway that included a child of seven.)

When the curtain rose, the actors were tense, and Mary Blair was especially nervous. But as the play progressed, the actors warmed to their roles, and the audience sat attentively, straining to hear every word. When Mary knelt at Paul's knee and brushed her lips to his wrist, the audience did not react at all. The gesture—and the evening—was, in O'Neill's words, "a dreadful anti-climax for all concerned, particularly the critics who seemed to feel cheated that there hadn't been at least one murder."[7]

Critical reaction to the play was generally unfavorable. "Long and wordy," sighed Robert Benchley, though noting the "powerful idea behind it." The *Afro-American* found it a "hard play to sit through . . . To see a big, respectable and cultured character as the slave of a slim, depraved and silly white woman isn't the kind of enjoyment calculated to make up a good evening's entertainment."

Paul's performance drew divided notices. Alexander Woollcott thought him "magnificent." George Jean Nathan remarked on his inexperience but concluded that he was "one of the most thoroughly eloquent, impressive and convincing actors that I have looked at and listened to in almost twenty years of professional theatregoing." And Laurence Stallings wrote with prescience in the *World*, "The man brings genius to the piece . . . And who has a better voice for tragedy than this actor, whose tone and resonance suggests nothing so much as the dusky, poetic quality of a Negro spiritual. . . ." But the *Brooklyn Eagle* thought he seemed like an uncomfortable student delivering a speech. Critical reaction notwithstanding, *Chillun* enjoyed a good run at Provincetown, playing in repertory with *The Emperor Jones* until October 10.

The summer marked a kind of turning point in Paul's life. When he had accepted the roles in O'Neill's plays, his main pursuit was still a law career, but the critical responses and his own private reaction to his performances changed things. He had been peripherally involved in the theater for years and found it fun, perhaps even liberating. Now any doubts about his acting ability or the possibility of a theatrical career were dispelled by his reception in *Jones* and *Chillun*. Some instinct convinced him he was on the right track; the law was not for him.

Paul was also attracted to the informality, camaraderie, and freewheeling intellectualism of the Provincetowners and their friends, characteristics that suited his own temperament precisely. He and Essie spent more and more time on Macdougal Street, in Village restaurants and parks, in the company of their newfound friends— actors, painters, writers—some of whom divided their time between writing and radical political activity.

One of the artists, Antonio Salemme, showed him how to look at and appreciate paintings and sculpted a lifesize bronze of Paul in the nude. Paul, in turn, introduced Salemme and his other friends to records of Bessie Smith and Ethel Waters, his favorite singers.

Quickly Paul and Essie's circle of friends broadened to include some of the most noted intellectuals of New York. Alexander Woollcott, who had panned Paul's performance in *Taboo* a few years earlier and met him briefly then, gave him a rave review for *The Emperor Jones* and promptly invited him to a party. The fledgling friendship nearly fizzled when Woollcott caught Paul mixing scotch with ginger ale, but eventually Paul and Essie became intimates of Woollcott's, and Alexander and Paul remained close friends until the critic's death.

Another of Paul's early friendships in the literary world was with Heywood Broun. The Brouns entertained many prominent blacks in their house on Eighty-fifth Street—among them James Weldon Johnson, Walter White, Jules Bledsoe, Rosalind Johnson, and Florence Mills. Paul, however, was an especially welcome guest because at times he was the only one who could get young Woodie Broun to go to bed. He would hoist the boy on his shoulders and sing a spiritual or a folk song.

The Robeson's widening social circle naturally included the most promising members of the Harlem Renaissance. Paul and Essie were frequent guests at the lavish parties given on 136th Street or at Irvington-on-Hudson by A'Lelia Walker, heiress of Madame C. J. Walker, who had made millions through processing and treatment of Negro women's hair. A'Lelia Walker welcomed artists, writers, musicians, and sculptors to her parties, and at her house Paul could find Countee Cullen, Langston Hughes, Arna Bontemps, and James Weldon Johnson. She also entertained agents, producers, and publishers, because she wanted to give aspiring artists an opportunity to meet people who could help them.

A frequent such guest was Carl Van Vechten, of whom Mrs. James Weldon Johnson said, he "was a force, a spur in a labyrinth of individual effort, but for that which was already in process . . . he recognized it first, and he dramatized it." A writer himself, Van Vechten later said that in 1924 he became "violently interested in Negroes" almost to the point of "an addiction." That was the year that he became close friends with Walter White, who had just published *The Fire in the Flint.* Through White Van Vechten soon knew "every educated person in Harlem." Paul was among this number.

Despite his growing renown, Paul found money short after the close of *Jones* and *Chillun.* So he was receptive when, in the fall, Oscar Michaux, one of the most prolific of the independent, black movie-makers, approached him to make *Body and Soul,* a "race movie" intended primarily for black audiences. Paul played the lead, a rakehell Georgia Negro preacher whose secretive behavior suggests that he is concealing another identity. It was definitely a B movie, and Paul, who had taken the silent film role to make a little money and to get work as an actor, never referred to it, although *Variety* "was impressed with its power for both black and white audiences."[8] Contemporary film historian Donald Bogle has said, "Robeson without his voice was merely beautiful and mysterious."[9]

The money he earned was enough to tide him over to December, when he received another opportunity to perform. At the invitation of a New York radio station, he sang a few spirituals and acted a scene from *The Emperor Jones* over the air, marking the first time any segment of an O'Neill play had been broadcast. Then several months passed without an offer of a suitable acting role. He was becoming discouraged. Essie continued her work as a pathologist at the Presbyterian Hospital of the Columbia Medical Center, and she kept on encouraging Paul. Years later she described his next step as "a natural one." The events that determined it began one day in late March 1925. Paul was standing alone on the corner of 135th Street and Seventh Avenue. Suddenly his face lit up. Approaching him was the slight figure of Lawrence Brown, whom Paul hadn't seen since 1922 when he was in London for his role in *Voodoo.* Brown had returned to the States to visit his ailing father, who recently had died in Philadelphia; he was staying with friends across the street from where Paul stood. The chance meeting delighted Robeson, who told

Brown how much he had liked the volume of spirituals Brown had sent him. He asked him to come to Jimmy Light's home in the Village that evening. "We might play some songs," he said offhandedly.

Paul had been singing for small groups of friends for some time, and had even sung professionally to help pay his way through law school. As far back as 1922 he had told Alexander Woollcott that he had discovered he had a pretty good voice. In the summer of 1924 when the Provincetowners had taken *The Emperor Jones* to Peterborough, New Hampshire, he had, at Jimmy Light's suggestion, replaced the whistling designated in the script with "a little snatch of Negro music." His singing was so successful then that he went back to Peterborough in early November to give a concert devoted entirely to black music. It was a natural request. Nearly everyone who had heard him sing in private urged him to give a public concert, but Paul hesitated because he had never had any training. Woollcott and Broun even took their case to Essie, arguing that no training was needed for folk songs the way he sang them. But unsure of what their commercial success would be, Paul had continued to demur until the Peterborough recital.

America was in the middle of the Jazz Age, but a Jazz Age that had been largely taken over by white musicians. Already in 1922 the white "King of Jazz," Paul Whiteman, was grossing more than a million dollars a year by appropriating black music, while black musicians, who originated it, were starving.[10] As for spirituals, they had fallen into disrepute during the years after emancipation, especially among intellectual blacks who saw them as an uncomfortable reminder of slavery, though here and there were signs that this might be changing. W. E. B. Du Bois had written that he considered spirituals to be a strong cultural link between the ancient past and the unknown future. And as early as the turn of the century, Harry T. Burleigh, J. Rosamond Johnson, James Weldon Johnson, and now Lawrence Brown were collecting and scoring them.

At Light's that evening, Robeson sang two of Brown's arrangements, "Swing Low, Sweet Chariot" and "Every Time I Feel the Spirit." Spontaneously, Brown joined in with his light tenor. It was electrifying. Jimmy Light immediately suggested that they give a public concert. Urged on by Essie, who wanted Paul to work with Larry Brown, and Walter White and many other friends both in Harlem and downtown, who thought a concert of all-Negro music important, Paul agreed.

The concert was hurriedly scheduled for April 19, the first Sunday

after Easter, at the Greenwich Village Theater. With only three weeks
to prepare, Paul and Essie's friends began feverishly working to make
it a success: Carl Van Vechten nailed up posters, passed out handbills,
and encouraged his friends to attend. Heywood Broun drummed up
interest through his column and Walter White ballyhooed the concert
through the Associated Negro Press. On the evening of April 19, the
theater was sold out.

The last Paul and Larry were nervous. Everything—Paul's voice, their
program, the audience—seemed cause for concern. Jimmy Light joked
backstage to relieve the tension, but Paul and Larry were still terrified
when they strode onto the stage to open with Harry T. Burleigh's
arrangement of "Go Down Moses."

The last deep note was greeted by thunderous applause. Paul then
went on to sing, "I Don't Feel No Ways Tired," "Weepin' Mary," "Bye
and Bye," and "Steal Away," until, in what seemed to be a spontaneous
response to the music, Larry joined in for his arrangement of "Every
Time I Feel De Spirit." The enthusiastic reception to the songs
dispelled any qualms Paul and Larry might have had, and they soon
forgot their anxiety, singing so beautifully and naturally that at the
end of the program, the audience simply refused to leave, applauding
and calling for more. Paul and Larry sang enough encores to make up
another concert, but it was only when Jimmy Light ordered the house
lights turned up that the audience consented to go home.

The critics raved. "Paul Robeson's singing is difficult to describe. It is
a voice in which deep bells ring. Mr. Brown is a craftsman," said the
New York World. "Mr. Robeson is a singer of genuine power. . . . His
Negro spirituals hold in them a cry from the depths, a universal
humanism which touches the heart," wrote the New York Times. "If
Feodor Chaliapin were so consummate an artist that he could transfer
his dramatic conception of the Russian song to the more childlike
emotion of Negro spirituals, he would try to sing them as Paul
Robeson does," wrote the New York Evening Post.

The concert had made history, for although choral groups like the
Fisk Jubilee Singers and the Hall Johnson Choir had sung concerts of
spirituals before, Robeson's was the first solo concert made up entirely
of Negro music to have received such attention. With the acclaim came
other opportunities. Paul, who found he enjoyed singing and reveled
in the newfound financial security it brought him, gave a second
concert at the Greenwich Village Theater a few weeks later. Shortly
afterward the Pond Bureau signed him and Brown for a concert tour,

offering them 55 percent of the income and promising that Paul could be free for theatrical engagements during part of the season. Essie quit her job at Columbia Hospital to act as road manager, and they borrowed $5,000 from Otto Kahn against their Pond earnings to get their affairs in order.

Recordings were the next step. Bypassing the black star system that already existed for blues singers such as Bessie Smith and Ma Rainey (who appealed chiefly to blacks), Paul looked for a way to capitalize on his wide appeal to both races. In May he signed a recording contract with Victor Talking Machine Company.

There was just time to do a play before the concert tour scheduled in early 1926, so in August, four hectic months after that first recital, Paul and Essie were on their way to London.

V:
Ascent to Fame

The *Emperor Jones*, directed by Jimmy Light and with Harold McGhee as stage manager, was scheduled to open at the Ambassadors Theatre in London in September 1925. Paul was in a buoyant mood; Brutus Jones was "a great part,"[1] he thought, and he was glad to be playing it in London. More important, the idleness between acting roles was over. Even now, Larry was traveling in the South, collecting new spirituals for their first full-fledged concert tour. Meanwhile, there would be plenty to do, if the play ran until December as expected.

Londoners flocked to see the much-talked-about American drama starring a black man. After all, it had been well over fifty years since Ira Aldridge had been engaged to play Othello at the Lyceum. Once inside the theater, however, the reaction was mixed. Some of the audience sat gripped and intent as O'Neill's psychological drama unfolded, but many of those present seemed troubled and restless. The incessant beating of the tom-toms, even between the scenes when the curtain was down, threw the Britons into a frenzy. "Maddening," "persistent," "terrifying," they said—the exact effect that O'Neill intended, but troubling to the audience nonetheless.

The critics were, on the whole, divided in their reaction to O'Neill's drama, and some reviewers and feature writers thought the production freakish. "London is being entertained by all sorts of imported actors of genius," twittered the *Star*. "One day it is a French midget . . . who plays a monkey, and the next it is a coloured giant . . . without his shoes. . . ."

The more favorable reviews generally lauded Paul for his presence and dignity, his voice and his acting, which he found especially amusing. "I couldn't understand what they were talking about. I knew nothing about the technique of acting, or about the actor's art."[2]

Nevertheless, he was pleased with the compliments. He was even more pleased with life in London and the apparent lack of discrimination there. Though the play closed early in October, contrary to hopes, Paul and Essie decided to stay at their flat at 24 Cheyne Row in Chelsea, so Paul could get a much-needed rest. They had already made new friends: Carl Van Vechten had sent a letter of introduction to Hugh Walpole, who invited Paul to lunch; world traveler Ralph Stock had invited Essie and Paul to parties on his yacht. They looked forward to spending some time with such friends as the Johnstones, of the black American dance team Layton and Johnstone, and with John Payne, the Alabama-born baritone whom Robeson had stayed with on his last London trip. Payne, renowned for his rendition of spirituals, was the protégé of Lady Cooke, and his luxurious flat in Regents Park was "a society meeting place for tea, cocktails and soirees."3

Among the other people the Robesons met was Emma Goldman, the Russian-born anarchist who had been deported from the United States with 248 other Russians during the Red Scare in 1919. She invited the Robesons to dinner, and Essie was touched when she told them of her "disheartening experiences" in Russia. It was tragic, Essie felt, that such a big-hearted woman was isolated in London "with only the few crumbs of news brought by occasional visitors from America to cheer her."4

As the weather in London turned cold and misty the Robesons began to think about returning to the United States, but just when they were about to leave, Glenway Westcott, the writer, invited them to Villefranche-sur-Mer in southern France. Not really anxious to return home right away, Paul and Essie joined the growing group of American writers and artists on the Riviera.

In the small village between Nice and Monte Carlo Paul and Essie could relax in the sunshine. Paul swam and fished, and whenever the fancy struck them, they visited the surrounding countryside and neighboring towns. In Nice one day Paul ran into black poet Claude McKay, whom he had known in Harlem. McKay introduced Paul to his friend Max Eastman, editor (with Floyd Dell) of *The Masses*, who was in Nice finishing up a book. He and McKay had traveled to Russia together, and they spent long hours talking to Paul about socialism and their experiences in Russia.

Paul and Essie also met opera singer Mary Garden and novelists Rebecca West and G.B. Stern, who thought Villefranche-sur-Mer "the one place worth living in which British and American tourists haven't invaded." Gertrude Stein, to whom Carl Van Vechten had written to announce "the approach of two of the nicest people left in the world: Essie and Paul Robeson," gave a party for them. "Paul interested Gertrude Stein," wrote the author in *The Autobiography of Alice B. Toklas*. "He knew American values and American life as only one in it but not of it could know them. And yet as soon as any other person came into the room he became definitely a Negro. Gertrude Stein did not like hearing him sing spirituals. They do not belong to you any more than anything else, so why claim them? she said. He did not answer."

Gertrude Stein notwithstanding, the Robesons returned to New York three days before Christmas to prepare for Paul's first extended concert tour. The Pond Bureau billed him "The Music Sensation of the Season," and he lived up to that promise with his opening Town Hall concert in New York on January 5, 1926.

Again and again he and Larry Brown performed for full houses as the tour swung across the East Coast and through the Midwest. Critics praised Paul and Larry as forming "an almost perfect blend," and described Paul as one of the most satisfying interpreters of Negro music. A Boston critic, comparing him to Roland Hayes, wrote that because Paul's voice was more natural, he attracted more Negroes to his concerts. Still, most of Paul's audiences were composed of "hypercritical whites," whom he won over time and time again.

The success of the tour was marred only by the discrimination that Paul, Essie, and Larry encountered. It was especially painful to Paul who liked to think that when he was singing or acting, race prejudice was forgotten. "Art is one form against which such barriers do not stand," he used to say. Like other Harlem intellectuals at the time he had an intense desire to believe in America and its promises. Yet he found that away from the footlights, he still could not eat in a decent restaurant from Tenth to 125th Streets. He and white producers were frequently turned away from midtown restaurants. At one lunch in his honor the management set up a table in the basement of the restaurant, although ironically when Paul sang after lunch, the patrons nearly emptied the main dining room and crowded into the cellar.

Even stopping by to see friends could cause embarrassment. Because of his frequent visits to Konrad Bercovici, Paul learned, the Rumanian writer's neighbors had objected, and he had been forced to move. On tour there was constant trouble with hotels, theaters, trains, even restrooms. Once in Boston Paul, Essie, and Larry were turned away from a modest hotel at which they had reserved rooms in advance. They drove around in a taxi for several hours trying to decide what to do, until Essie directed the driver to the Copley Plaza, the best hotel in town. She asked for rooms there and got them. But by the time they got to the concert hall Paul, who had caught a cold on the drafty overnight train from New York, was much worse. He gave the worst concert of his fledgling career.

Because of these experiences Paul had no illusions about the difficulties a black actor faced. Audiences preferred "to see Al Jolson or Frank Tinney blacken his face and imitate us," he said. Nevertheless, Paul's triumphs in the O'Neill plays and his growing fame as a singer heightened interest in him as an actor. He had been mentioned for the role of Othello as early as 1924 (though he resented this automatic typecasting, and felt, besides, that *Othello* should be the climax of a career). And he dreamed of doing a great play, maybe about Haiti, written and acted by Negroes, a moving drama that would have none of the themes that offer targets for racists. He also aspired to nonracial parts, hoping that the trend away from theatrical realism would help him get them.

But his next role was both racial and realistic. Soon after he returned to New York from his concert tour, Horace Liveright announced plans for *Black Boy*, starring Paul Robeson.

The play, by Jim Tully and Frank Dazey, is about the rise and fall of Black Boy, a vagrant who reluctantly becomes a prizefighter. He wins the championship, only to be felled by riotous living and betrayed by his mistress. Deserted by the girl when it is clear that he has lost his crown, Black Boy discovers that "his little white missy" was really black, and that his whole world was an elaborate illusion.

Black Boy opened at Broadway's Comedy Theater on October 6 to lukewarm reviews. Paul fared somewhat better at the hands of the reviewers—Brooks Atkinson called his performance "a fine-grained, resilient bit of characterization." But he felt he had compromised in playing the role, and he was ashamed of it later. Certainly, the part crystalized for him the contradictory strains a black actor faced: On the one hand, Negroes could not be presented realistically in the theater. On the other, Robeson was getting "that rare chance for a Negro actor—a starring role." So it was understandable if he did not pay as much attention to the vehicle for that opportunity as he should have. Meanwhile, Paul was emerging increasingly as a symbol of what blacks might achieve. Elizabeth Shepley Sargeant, writing in *The New Republic*, said of him: "(He) is not merely an actor and a singer of Negro spirituals but a symbol. A sort of sublimation of what the Negro may be in the Golden Age hangs about him, and imparts to his appearances an atmosphere of affection and delight that is seldom felt in an American audience."

After *Black Boy* closed, Paul gave Sunday night concerts in early December at the Comedy Theater, playing to capacity houses, and in April 1927 he sang again at Town Hall before embarking on his concert tour. That spring, however, Essie's familiar figure was missing at the out-of-town concerts. She stayed home because she was pregnant.

In the summer Paul was asked to play opposite Mrs. Patrick Campbell again in a London revival of *Taboo*. He was reluctant to leave Essie—although her mother was now staying with her—but the Robesons needed the money. Assured that Essie would be all right, he left for London in the fall. The opening of the play was marred by bad news from home. Paul's oldest brother, Bill, a Washington, D.C., doctor, had suddenly taken ill and died. Of the family, only Marion, a teacher in Philadelphia, had been with him at the end.

From London Paul, joined by Larry Brown, crossed the Channel, and Paul sang for the first time in Paris at the Maison Gaveau. The French press and public raved. Paul saw this as indication "that people, no matter what their race or nationality, find something of a high order in [black] music."[5]

On November 2, 1927, while Paul was in Paris, Essie gave birth to Paul, their only child. Always of indifferent health, she nearly died in childbirth. Her mother stayed on to help while she recovered, and when Essie returned to her more strenuous and time-consuming chores as Paul's manager, Mrs. Goode became a permanent part of the household. She was to look after the boy throughout much of his childhood.

Paul's search for a suitable stage role continued. Early in 1928 he replaced Jack Carter as Crown in *Porgy*, the play by DuBose and Dorothy Heyward about the inhabitants of Catfish Row. He left the role after only a month, however, because he found singing the blues put too great a strain on his voice.

Then an offer that had been under discussion intermittently since 1926 was firmed up. When Jerome Kern, who had been working on a stage version of Ferber's book *Show Boat*, composed "Ol' Man River," with words by Oscar Hammerstein, he knew right away that the song was tailor-made for Robeson. Kern had telephoned Alexander Woollcott, who put him in touch with Paul and Essie, and had raced up to Harlem with the song. In fact, Paul liked it and agreed to appear in *Show Boat*, but other commitments intervened. Now, two years later, when he was offered the role of Joe in the London production of the play, he was in a position to accept. So in the spring of 1928 he and Essie left young Pauli with his grandmother and embarked once more for London.

Rehearsals started in April on what was to be one of Drury Lane's biggest productions. Costing some $30,000, the play would have a cast of more than 160 people, wearing over 1,000 costumes. But excitement over the play was clouded when, in the midst of the rehearsals for *Show Boat*, Paul received a wire asking him to return to New York. Before accepting the role in the Kern musical, he had signed a contract with a Mrs. Caroline Dudley Reagan to star in a revue that would "reflect Negro ideals and viewpoints with accuracy." He had been paid in advance but nothing more had been heard about the project in the ensuing months. Now Mrs. Reagan was asking him to honor the contract. Paul refused. He had entered into the contract, he said, when Essie was ill, without being fully aware of all that was involved. He now felt incapable of performing in Mrs. Reagan's revue.

The dispute went on for months, even during the actual run of *Show Boat*. Paul returned the advance, but Mrs. Reagan brought suit against him, and Actors Equity in New York slapped a suspension on him. The punishment was in effect only in America and covered only Paul's acting, but it had racial overtones that reverberated throughout the black community. Alarmed, Walter White cabled Paul in London, "Reaction already very bad. Feel will hurt you and all of us." But the English columnist Hannon Swaffer commented, "It seems to me a pity to drag Mr. Robeson's color into this question." Mrs. Reagan also sought an injunction to stop Paul from appearing in the English *Show Boat*, but Sir Alfred Butt of the Drury Lane declared that Robeson's departure from the show would be disastrous. The injunction was denied. The matter was finally settled a year later, when a court awarded damages to Mrs. Reagan.

Whatever Paul's other reasons for refusing to star in Mrs. Reagan's show, artistic considerations seemed to play an important role. "I must work out my career as an artist. . . . My own black people blame me for

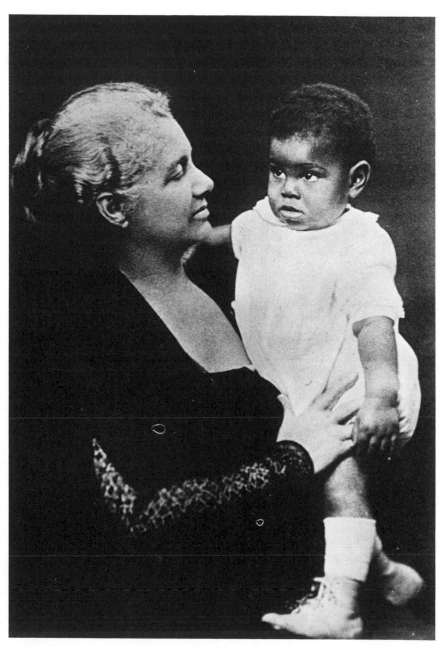

Essie's mother, Mrs. Goode, and Paul Robeson, Jr.

letting them down. . . . I cannot sing blues. It was all a mistake."[6] The same month Equity quoted Essie, who had returned to New York to help straighten out the matter, as saying that Paul did not consider himself an actor anyway, but a singer.[7]

Show Boat opened at the Drury Lane on May 3, 1928, with a plot that revolved around the people who live on Captain Andy's steamboat, *Cotton Blossom*: the stars of the troop, Julie and Steve; Captain Andy's daughter Magnolia; and Gaylord Ravenal, a professional gambler. In the background of the major action—the discovery of Julie's Negro blood and her forced departure from the show boat, Ravenal's marriage to Magnolia, the birth of their daughter, and his desertion— is the ever-present figure of Joe, the black riverman. His song, "Ol' Man River" was the best known and most popular in the show, which drew fine notices for its music, scenery, and sumptuous costumes. Several reviewers thought its "inspired eccentricity" and "charm" made up for what it lacked in humor. Paul's rendition of "Ol' Man River" was singled out; however, the black press did not join in the general praise for the play. There were favorable comments on Paul's performance, but sharp criticism of the stereotype he portrayed. Paul did not comment publicly at the time, but he told friends that he would someday have his own theater and produce plays *he* wanted.

The response to Paul's singing in *Show Boat* led Sir Alfred Butt to experiment with Sunday afternoon recitals at Drury Lane. Larry Brown came over from Paris to accompany him, and the first recital filled the house. Others followed there in close succession.

In the fall of 1928 Paul and Essie decided to settle permanently in London. *Show Boat*'s predicted long run and Paul's suspension by Actors Equity, which would temporarily prevent his working on the American stage, undoubtedly figured in this decision. Then, too, an extensive European tour was planned. But among the chief motivations for settling in England was, as Paul put it, the same reasons as those which had over the years brought blacks out of the American South.

The Robesons were now living in Hampstead, facing the Heath, in what the poet Hart Crane, who visited them late that year, described as a "sumptuous home rented from an ex-Ambassador to Turkey."[8] One entered it from an old-fashioned English garden and mounted stone steps. A winding stairway led to a second-floor sitting room with solid chairs and book-lined walls. Paul's room adjoined the library;

Essie's was on the same floor at the back. It was there, seated at an enormous desk, before French windows overlooking the park, that she transacted all of Paul's business. Paul and Essie soon brought Mrs. Goode and Pauli over, and then the first-floor drawing room was converted into a playroom for the boy. To run the house Essie engaged a staff of servants, including a French butler, although Paul's tastes in most things were simpler.

Now the Robesons were increasingly drawn into London's political, intellectual, and social circles. In late 1928 a group of Labour MPs invited Paul to lunch at the House of Commons and seated him next to Ramsay MacDonald who talked to him about Britain's colonies and Socialism. "I accepted the invitation," he explained, "but I didn't know anything about Socialism," Paul said. "I didn't realize that Socialism was something most people did know something about. . . ."[9]

Some weeks later he went to lunch with a British friend of Larry Brown's to meet Bernard Shaw. Mrs. Calvin Coolidge was seated on one side of the writer, and she reacted "loudly and aggressively" when Shaw talked about Socialism. Paul, however, was speechless when Shaw asked his opinion on the subject. "I'd never really thought about Socialism,"[10] he claimed.

Paul's statement is at variance with glimpses of his earlier life. Socialism, of course, had long been discussed in New York circles, and many of Paul's New York friends were radicals. William Patterson recalled that he, Robeson, and Heywood Broun talked "often" of the subject. Essie, too, in her account of Paul's chance meeting with Claude McKay and Max Eastman in 1928, wrote that "Paul listened eagerly to the talk about Russia and Socialism." Possibly, what Robeson meant was that his knowledge was superficial. Certainly at this point he had not developed his ideas on the subject.

Social London lionized Paul. He was asked to tea by Sir William and Lady Rothenstein of the Royal College of Art, and staunch imperialists such as Lord Beaverbrook invited him to sing at their receptions. Beaverbrook, writes historian A. J. P. Taylor, liked background noise and often offended the members of the chamber music ensembles he invited to play for him by talking during the performances. "Paul Robeson received a more appreciative welcome and came four times in succession, at a fee of eighty-four pounds, 10 shillings for each recital—a large sum for those days."[11] In June 1929 Paul accompanied Essie and actress Pola Negri to lunch at Lord Beaverbrook's. The occasion was recorded by another guest in his diary with the remarks,

"(Robeson) is a pleasant enough Negro whose ambition it is to play Othello in straight drama. Robeson danced with all the white women."[12]

The Robesons were gratified by the seeming ease of their contacts with the British monied class. Paul felt that he was treated "as a gentleman and a scholar. My background at Rutgers and my interest in academic studies was given much more weight than such matters are given in America," he said. He was also impressed with what he considered to be a higher sense of justice among the British, and he appreciated the respect for law and order "common throughout the British Isles."

In the spring of 1929 Paul, Larry, and Essie toured Central Europe for the first time, beginning in the Musikvereinsaal in Vienna on April 10. Robeson was already known to continental audiences through his recordings, but that was not the same thing as seeing him in person. The novelty of it was not to be missed, but his artistry also charmed the critical Viennese audience. "People wanted to see a Negro—they wanted to see how a Negro sings; and they suddenly felt themselves assisting at an important artistic event. The cheap sensation did not materialize," reported Siegfried Geyer in *Die Stunde*.

It was in Vienna that Robeson's growing political consciousness became more focused. A young music lover had invited Paul to his home after the concert, and Paul accepted the next day. Though the host had said he was very poor, Paul was totally unprepared for what he found: He would "never forget" the poverty he saw that day. Nor how shocked he was to find that his host's mother was a very cultured woman. "I couldn't understand people like that living in such poverty. I knew they were Jewish, but at the time, I didn't understand the position of the Jewish people in Europe."[13]

After Vienna Paul, Essie, and Larry went on to Budapest, where critics applauded him. In Prague the party was warmly welcomed by Lewis Einstein, the American minister to Czechoslovakia, who entertained them at the legation and provided an official car to take them to Smetana Hall. This treatment contrasted sharply with what they received from the American Embassy in London, where the Robesons had never even been invited to the annual Fourth of July parties.

After a few weeks on the Continent Paul returned to England to make his first appearance at Albert Hall. Whether by design or accident, it was scheduled for April 28, the anniversary of his opening appearance in *Show Boat*, and thousands of people filled the large auditorium. The critics were, as usual, laudatory, though the *Evening Standard* wondered when Paul would broaden his repertory to "a more sophisticated type" of song. The reviewer need not have worried about the programs becoming monotonous. When Paul toured British spas and seaside resorts that summer—on a percentage basis to prove that he could reach new audiences—listeners refused to leave after the final encores.

It was one day not long after that Paul walked into the offices of his manager, Lionel Powell, and was introduced to F. C. Coppicus, the famous impresario and director of New York's Metropolitan Musical Bureau. "I am pleased to meet you, Mr. Robeson, and I hereby engage you for the United States and Canada," he said. Coppicus, who had managed the tours of Caruso, Chaliapin, Rosa Ponselle, and Jeritza, had never met him and never heard him sing, but he had seen Paul in *The Emperor Jones*. He had never met a man of any race who had as many talents as Paul, Coppicus said. He acted on that admiration. On September 8, 1929, he signed Paul to a long-term contract.

The successes Robeson had experienced abroad were repeated a few months later as he toured the United States—beginning with a Carnegie Hall concert—under his new arrangement with Coppicus. It helped him forget about a deeply disturbing incident that had occurred just before his departure from England.

Paul and Essie had arrived for a midnight drink with an English friend at the Grill Room of the Savoy Hotel and been turned away. Paul had never experienced anything like this before in England, and he was stunned. He "sent for the manager, who informed me that . . . the management did not permit Negroes to enter the rooms any longer." As word of the incident quickly spread, Africans and West Indians became aroused. Labour MP James Marley raised the matter in the House of Commons; and Ramsay MacDonald, now Prime Minister, expressed mild concern, but refused to intervene.

Though the magic of his talent had put him in a special category— "darling blacks" the English called people like him—it was clear that England was no haven from racial discrimination. If even for someone of Paul Robeson's fame, the color bar still existed, how much more bigotry must striving students and other working-class blacks face? Perhaps he must cast his lot with them. The Savoy incident etched itself in Robeson's racial consciousness; it became a turning point in the development of his attitude and feelings toward England.

VI:
A Marriage in
Trouble

By 1930, hardly five years after choosing the theater and the concert stage as a career, Paul Leroy Robeson was an international celebrity. Now thirty-two years old, he was a powerful, somewhat shy-appearing giant of a man, whose handsome Negroid features were almost immediately recognized in America, England, and on the Continent. Official recognition for him varied from place to place. The British *Who's Who* detailed his entire career for publication the following year. By contrast, the American *Who's Who* omitted any reference to him whatever. Jacob Epstein, the famous sculptor, carved his head in stone and wood—the head of a man of undetermined age, tilted upward with eyes staring fixedly into the horizon. But the Art Alliance of Philadelphia refused to exhibit the nude bronze of him sculpted five years earlier by Antonio Salemme, because of their "apprehension of the consequences of exhibiting such a figure in a public square, especially the figure of a colored man, as the colored problem seems to be unusually great in Philadelphia."

In London Paul had a host of female admirers and, as a man who later became an intimate recalls, like many other great, handsome men he was not insensitive to the opportunities for affairs. "I think women occupied second place but they were always there . . . always there," the friend remembered.[1]

Essie—capable, assertive, and ambitious to be a person in her own right—knew there were other women in her husband's life, but she loved Paul and chose to ignore them. They both felt the additional strain of her delicate health and of long separations while he toured. Essie, often lonely and ever conscious of her roots in the black aristocracy, had few real confidantes and preferred to mask her real feelings with a smile or a bon mot. For his part, Paul was deeply dependent on her, not only emotionally but also in his career. She handled most of his business affairs and took care of his voluminous correspondence. "I want to make a good job of Paul and little Paul, but it's a whole-time job," Essie told a reporter from the *Daily Express*. Still, she found time to write, *Paul Robeson, Negro,* which appeared late in May.

Geared to a British audience, the book was at times offensive in its simplistic explanations of complex racial phenomena and revealed a certain limited sensitivity to Paul's essential nature. But because Essie had helped to direct Paul's career and had been on hand at many of the events she wrote about, the book was a valuable record. Most surprising and revealing were the glimpses it provided of their marriage. Though tacitly admitting knowledge of Paul's affairs, Essie described him as faithful "in the all important spirit of things" but "very lazy." Strong feelings, mutual strengths and admiration, an underlying air of mistrust, coyness, and a sense of incompatibility emerged as the chief components of their relationship, and publication of the book provoked loud protests from many quarters about the harm it might do to Paul. Essie dismissed these as coming from "white feminine admirers—women who are jealous of me and who became angrier yet when I laughed at them in the book."[2]

Paul was upset by the book. Essie discussed him as if he was her possession and somehow mentally inferior. Essie, one intimate said, "was convinced of one thing—that women were superior to men rather than equal. Essie liked women better than she liked men." By contrast, Paul was not a male chauvinist. His liking and respect for women as equal human beings was genuine. "Not all of the women who were fond of him wanted to go to bed with him nor he with them. He had a great capacity for friendship."[3]

In March Paul made his first trip to Germany to do *The Emperor Jones* at Berlin's Künstler Deutsches Theatre. The English-language production was directed by James Light, and Paul was hailed by German critics. On his return to London Paul began rehearsals for the role he once thought should climax his career. He had been preparing for *Othello* ever since September 1929, when, reluctant at first, he had finally signed a contract with Maurice Browne, the prominent

American actor-producer. Paul got to know Sir Frank Benson and at the Shakespearean actor's country home, spent hours listening to him talk about the Shakespearean traditions and the playwright. He read everything he could about the subject, as well as books on phonetics, and he listened to records so that he could enunciate in "good honest English" with no trace of an American accent.[4]

The rhythm of Shakespeare's verse appealed to the singer in him, so for help in his interpretation of Othello as a "fine" and "noble" character he had gone to Amanda Ira Aldridge, the voice coach and daughter of Ira Aldridge, the black actor who had played *Othello* in England and Europe so successfully in the nineteenth century. Paul saw Othello as "an alien . . . among the white people . . . facing a highly developed white civilization, . . . a great general . . . but yet in a precarious position because of his race."[5] "We always hear that Othello's jealousy is not believable; it comes too quickly. But I feel that is because he is not presented as of a different race, as Shakespeare intended, so that he feels himself apart. . . . It is very important because if the jealousy is not believable then the whole tragedy falls to pieces."[6]

The rehearsals for *Othello* were an "extraordinary" experience for Paul that increased his love of the theater. But there were days when he was so fearful that he could hardly rise from his bed. Ellen Van Volkenberg Browne, who directed her husband's production, recalled Essie's calling one morning to report that Paul said he was too sick to get up. Essie asked Mrs. Van Volkenberg to come to their home. Together they confronted Paul and finally got him up. "Essie drove to the theater and Paul sat between the two of us," Mrs. Van Volkenberg recalled nearly fifty years later. By the time rehearsals ended, Paul could say enthusiastically, "Now I want to act." Maurice Browne recalls that, "Night after night, unaccompanied, by the light of a great log-fire in the music-room Robeson sang 'spirituals' . . . He spoke blank verse, particularly the long speeches, almost as well as he sang . . . His movement was not always good, but his emotional power was terrifying. In the 'jealousy' scenes he—literally—foamed at the mouth; I used to wonder whether one day he might not seize Iago and pluck out my arm."[7]

Othello opened at the Savoy Theatre on May 19 with Peggy Ashcroft, a promising young actress whom Paul and Essie had seen in *Jew Suss*, cast as Desdemona; Ralph Richardson, just beginning his climb to fame, was Roderigo, and the talented Sybil Thorndike, Emilia. Paul was understandably nervous. During rehearsals, a number of threatening letters had protested his being cast against a white woman, and these had shaken him so that at first he had refused to get close to Peggy Ashcroft. His opening-night jitters, exacerbated by a legitimate fear of racism, seemed, to some, to result in his not knowing what to do with his hands and arms; even his fingers seemed to twitch. But as the play progressed he quickly dominated his scenes, and from the moment the last lines of the play were spoken, cries for Paul erupted from all parts of the theater. Twenty curtain calls were taken before the applause died down. "I'm so happy. I'm so happy," Paul said, sobbing with joy when asked to speak to the audience.

Reviewers had widely ranging views. Some criticized the cuts in the play and its condensation into four acts, the setting, and the noise the scenery made when it was shifted. Many considered Paul as "dominating the stage." "The most impressive Othello in a generation." A few reviewers asserted that Shakespeare had meant Othello to be a Moor and not a black African. It was a question that scholars had been debating for years. Paul was convinced that Shakespeare had a black man in mind. In fact, he felt that Othello was the universal black man in white society—tolerated when he was valuable, banished when he desired a white woman.

"In Shakespeare's time, I feel there was no great distinction between the Moor and the brown or black. Surely most of the Moors have Ethiopian blood and come from Africa, and to Shakespeare's mind he was called a blackamoor."[8]

Paul's success predictably enlarged his circle of friends, and one Britisher Paul met during the run of *Othello* was drama critic Marie Seton, who was later to become his biographer and confidante and friend to both him and Essie.

News of the new Moor quickly reached America, increasing the possibility that he would do Othello in the United States. Editorials in New York papers, however, strongly criticized the thought of such a venture, and Paul later agreed that America "wouldn't stand for the kissing and for the scene in which I use Miss Ashcroft roughly." In fact, he thought that if the production traveled, audiences in some parts of the country might become dangerous.

Othello closed in July, but by late August Paul was back at the Savoy, this time for a week of special programs, partly devoted to music and partly to extracts from *The Emperor Jones*. Audiences in London and in the provinces, where the show toured in September, were on the

Robeson as Othello and Peggy Ashcroft as Desdemona in the 1930 production
in London. Photo courtesy of Marie Seton.

whole exasperated by the experiment; they wanted more acting. But
the show gave Paul a chance to experiment and vary his music
somewhat, adding to his spirituals songs by Beethoven, Schumann,
and Mozart.

Paul's contact with Africans and West Indians in London was
causing him to rethink his music. He began to talk, not only of the
thematic Biblical origins of spirituals, but also of their African melodic
origins. He thought they related directly to Central Africa, that the
slaves took their melodies with them to America and there, influenced
by the Bible and the overseer's whip, they developed the spirituals.
Through the Moors, he thought, these melodies influenced European
composers such as Ravel as well. One alteration of African rhythm in
America produced jazz, he felt. "But jazz to my mind has no spiritual
significance. I do not think it will have any serious effect on Real
music."[9]

Borderline appeared at film societies in half a dozen European
countries shortly before the end of *Othello*. Paul had been curious
about film for some time, an interest that coincided with the current
fashion for avant-garde cinema groups in Britain and Europe. When
Kenneth McPherson, an experimental film-maker and editor of the
film journal *Close Up*, invited him to appear in a full-length feature for

which he had written the scenario, Paul agreed. The film was shot in Switzerland, and Paul played a stranger whose chance arrival starts a village tragedy. Essie acted the role of his estranged wife. According to McPherson's wife, the writer Bryher, "The only paid member of the group was an electrician. Extras had to be dispersed rather than sought, everybody wanted to be in it and every twenty minutes all the lights went out because the tram went by."[10] McPherson's story line was weak; he was most interested in cinematic technique. Yet the film showed blacks in human situations, rather than in the racially stereotyped ones that prevailed in Hollywood. The English were cool to *Borderline*, and it was never shown in American theaters at all. Years later, however, various exhibitors included it in examples of early avant-garde cinema.

By the end of 1930 Paul's personal life was in a shambles, and he and Essie abandoned attempts to keep up appearances. The strains hinted at in Essie's book reached the breaking point. She and Paul quietly separated.

About this time Paul took on a new representative, Robert Rockmore. Paul had met him first in 1924, with Provincetowner James Light, and again four years later when Rockmore was in London as a foreign dramatic correspondent. From 1931 on the trusted Rockmore supervised Paul's artistic, legal, financial and, sometimes, personal affairs.

Early in 1931 Paul came to the United States on a four-month concert tour. In Kansas City during an interview with Roy Wilkins, then a young reporter, he talked about his unhappy experiences of discrimination in New York the previous year and said that he would be rejoining Essie and Pauli when his tour ended in April. But this was only a cover. Paul had taken a flat at 19 Buckingham Street, Strand, above some offices, and Essie, Pauli, and Mrs. Goode had moved to Vienna. Essie thought that the Austrian capital would be easier on Paul, Jr., than London, where in Hampstead people would often touch the three-year-old boy's hair for luck. During the stay in Vienna she started work on a novel and on *Uncle Tom's Cabin*, a play about a black orchestra touring Europe.

A month after he returned to London, Paul opened in *The Hairy Ape*, his third O'Neill play, again directed by James Light. The role of Yank Smith, a stoker lost in the technological age, appealed to Paul, who saw him as a universal hero. The critics disagreed. After only five performances Paul had to withdraw because of laryngitis. The rehearsals had been killing, and if he didn't take a long rest, doctors told him, he might injure his voice permanently. Also the separation from Essie had interrupted the orderliness of his life, and though he was not the kind of father who enjoyed playing games with his four-year-old son, he missed the boy.

Paul was continuing to include a few classical works in his programs. But the classical selections in 1931 were not as well received as they had been the year before. Countee Cullen, who had attended Paul's recital with the Paris Symphony in the Salle Pleyel in 1930, recalled the nostalgia and pride he had felt listening to Paul's renditions of spirituals and German lieder. Cullen was not alone in his feelings. The audience then had shouted for encores, but the orchestra had no more of Paul's music. They yelled for him to sing without it. In deference to the musicians of the orchestra, Paul declined and ended the recital with a little speech of gratitude.

On the 1931 tour, however, only "The Prayer" by Gretchaninoff excited the reviewers. The reception for the song pleased Paul, who saw an affinity between the idiom of Russian and Negro songs. So did his audience. In New York, after a concert Russians and Jews had often crowded around him, saying that they too noticed a similarity. So Paul moved away from the classical works, away from the music he liked, and toward the Russian, Hebrew, and Balkan folk music that he "felt." He began studying Russian and German in earnest.

Late in November the *Daily Sketch* carried the following article:

> *Hundreds of women admirers besieged the stage door of the Palladium and mobbed Paul Robeson after his recital yesterday.*
>
> *They clutched him by the arm, thrust autograph books into his hand with cries of "You wonderful man," and clambered on to the footboard of his car until the police cleared a passage for him. . . .*

In 1932 Paul returned to America to appear in a revival of *Show Boat*. Though "Ol' Man River" had been written with him in mind, Paul had never sung the song in New York. Edna Ferber had thought it was too soon for a revival, and at first she refused to attend the opening night performance. But at the last minute she changed her mind, and went to the theater, only to witness a "mild riot" for seats. She had to stand in back behind the "fashionable" audience. When Paul appeared, the audience stood up and howled—applauded and shouted and stomped. She described what happened next in a letter to Alexander Woollcott. "Since then I have seen it exceeded but once, and that was when Robeson, a few minutes later, finished singing "Ol' Man River.""

The show stopped. He sang it again. The show stopped. They called him back again and again. Other actors came out and made motions and their lips moved, and the bravos of the audience drowned all other sounds."[11]

"It was during the run of *Show Boat* that the newspapers announced the Robesons' pending divorce. Paul had seen Essie and his son the previous Christmas, but apparently no reconciliation could be reached. He told a reporter that they had been separated for two years by mutual agreement, and "she has her career and I have mine." Essie, when questioned about the report, said, "I'm not giving the name of the corespondent because I don't know and I don't care who she is." She branded as "incredible" stories linking Paul with a famous titled Englishwoman. Their break was brought on by sheer ennui, she said; they had worked closely together for most of their eleven-year marriage. Now they wanted their freedom, but they would continue to be friends.[12]

Other rumors linked Paul with Nancy Cunard during his stay in New York. The daughter of Sir Bache and Lady Maude Cunard, of the shipping family, Nancy was in Harlem researching material for a book she was going to write on Negro life. The press implied that she and Paul were lovers, because they were both staying at the Hotel Theresa. In fact, she and Paul hardly knew each other. Intimates thought she was at the hotel with Henry Crowder, the black composer with whom she had been living in Paris since 1928, but even this wasn't true. Crowder had remained in Europe.

There was another woman in Paul's life, the friend of a friend of Marie Seton's. But Paul refused to name her and he was so outraged by the press stories that he contemplated taking legal action against the tabloids. He was quoted as telling reporters in New York that if he and his English mistress did marry, he would leave the United States because of racial problems. He would not be swayed by popular opinion.

Shortly afterward, Paul left the cast of *Show Boat* and returned to England. Before the divorce went through, Paul's love married someone else—a Frenchman. "He got his fingers burnt, and once was enough."[13] What happened between him and Essie during the next six months is not clear, for while Paul continued to admire her intellectual abilities and her courage, he never got over the book. Evidently they were reconciled, for during a visit to New York in February the following year, Essie was quoted as saying: "We are not going to divorce—ever. We are terribly happy."[14]

VII:
New Influences

In the early 1930s Paul started to feel the strains that would move him away from being a "pure" artist toward greater social and political awareness. By this time events of far-reaching consequence had occurred in Britain and the world. In 1931 the Depression that had swept through the United States had struck Britain, causing unemployment to soar to more than 2 million people. By the fall Britain had gone off the Gold Standard, leaving the economy shaky. In the same year, the Statute of Westminster aroused considerable controversy and sparked protest from Indians because it excluded their country from the dominion status given to Canada, Australia, New Zealand, and South Africa. Black African colonies were considered years removed from any form of self-government at all. But in London the West African Students Union was expressing militant opposition to colonialism, and the more moderate League of Coloured Peoples was founded in 1931 for the "welfare of coloured peoples in all parts of the world" and to better relations between the races.

From Germany the political news was growing more frightening. At the end of February 1933 the Reichstag burned, and the fire was blamed on the communists, in a move that consolidated Hitler's power. A month later when an enabling act gave the Nazis and their supporters complete control of Germany, Nazi persecution of political and racial minorities began in earnest. Leftists and non-Aryans, people like George Padmore, the West Indian Comintern agent, and Frederick Kuh, Jewish correspondent for an American news agency, began fleeing to England with tales of terror. There John Strachey, a leading spokesman for the Left, Victor Gollancz, the publisher, and James Maxton, the leader of the tiny Independent Labour Party and the man who had first taken Paul around the House of Commons nine years before, worked to rouse British socialists, trade unionists, and the Labour party to the menace of fascism.

Robeson's friend, anarchist Emma Goldman, campaigned to shame people into contributing money to organize a protest meeting, although what brought her the most notoriety in the early days of March was the literary luncheon held for her at Grosvenor House Hotel to celebrate publication of an English edition of *Living My Life*. Even the tributes of guests like Rebecca West, who spoke, and Paul, who sang "Sometimes I Feel Like a Mornin' Dove" and "Roll de Chariot Along," were overshadowed by what a Canadian paper called a "Deliberate Snub to King George."[1] The snub was the omission of the traditional toast to the king in deference to Goldman who threatened to leave if it were given.[2]

Gradually more attention was focused on the refugees themselves. James Maxton formed a joint committee with British communists, and on April 12 they sponsored a demonstration at Albert Hall to protest the Nazi regime and raise money for the refugees from Nazi terror.

Paul's immediate concern was still development of his artistry. In late 1932 he had begun dropping in at the Embassy Theatre at Swiss Cottage, which had been taken over by Ronald Adam, a former London accountant. With André van Gyseghem, a young actor who had tried his hand at producing, and Bagnall Harris, a set designer, both of whom had worked under the previous management, Adam produced mainly revivals. Van Gyseghem, who had always been interested in dramas of social and political problems, persuaded Paul to do *All God's Chillun* with Flora Robson as Ella.

The play was set to open in mid-March 1933. It almost closed during rehearsals, however, when quite unexpectedly Eugene O'Neill's agent demanded a thousand dollars advance on royalties, a sum the Embassy could not possibly afford. Even Paul and Flora Robson were getting only the usual ten pounds each. When Paul learned of the problem, he contributed 100 pounds toward the advance, but by opening night the advance bookings for *Chillun* were so great that Ronald Adam was able to return Paul's check. Though Paul's and Flora Robson's performances drew high praise, critical reaction to the play was generally unfavorable. Nevertheless, the production set box office records for the Embassy, and Adam arranged to give it a four weeks' special run at the Piccadilly. Paul continued to act for ten pounds a week, and Adam, who, in his own words, "was obsessed with the growing attractions of the cinema" drastically reduced the prices for seats. The policy boomeranged. Londoners, who would pay high prices to hear Robeson sing, assumed "there must be something wrong with Robeson, or the play, or the management, or the theatre that he should be presented at lower than normal theatre prices."[3]

One day during that spring of 1933 Marie Seton walked into his dressing room at the Piccadilly. Seton was always interested in social and racial problems; a few weeks before her visit she had accompanied André van Gyseghem to Moscow to help him obtain the rights of *Professor Mamlock* from Friedrich Wolf, who was in exile there. This evening she had come to ask Paul to do a benefit performance of *Chillun* for the German Jewish refugees in England.

During his first tour of Central Europe Paul had become vaguely aware of anti-Semitism. At that time he had concluded, "The Negro and the Jew have the same problems. . .Perhaps that's why I feel so close to the Jews. . ."[4] Once he had sharply told Seton that he had become interested in the Russian language not through White Russians in New York but through Russian Jews. "The white people who have been kindest to me in New York have been Jewish people," he said.[5] Later, when Seton had brought Frederick Kuh to interview him shortly before the opening of *Chillun*, Paul, shocked by Kuh's account of his escape and by Seton's description of the intimidation of German voters during the "election" in March, had expressed deep concern about the end of democracy in Germany. But a benefit performance was another matter. "I'm an artist. I don't understand politics," he told Seton, seeking to avoid controversy.

She answered that the sponsoring committee was headed by H.G. Wells and included James Marley, the man who had brought the Savoy Grill incident to the floor of the House of Commons. Every shade of political opinion was represented on the committee, and its members only wanted to help people who had been persecuted for the "crime of being Jews."

Paul was moved, but again he replied, "I've always avoided controversies. My province is art." Seton did not give up and hit on what was, for Paul, the convincing argument. She replied that he could never be simply an artist, that he would be reminded of his race as long as race prejudice existed. "Very well," he said sharply, "I'll play the matinee for the Jewish refugees." The benefit raised 2,000 pounds.[6]

May found Paul and Essie back in the United States for the filming of *The Emperor Jones*. Eugene O'Neill had been interested in a film version for a long time and had actually worked out a treatment for it as a silent film, "which would be equally good as a talky." But until he could be sure that Paul would play Brutus he had refused to sell the rights. Now, with Paul finally in the role he had made famous on the stage, the film was going to be produced by John Krimsky and Gifford Cochran, American sponsors of the German film classic, *Maedchen in Uniform*. *The Emperor Jones*, in which Krimsky and Cochran had invested a quarter of a million dollars, was their first film-producing venture, and they hoped it would lead to the emancipation of films from Hollywood control and a revival of the East as a center of film production. Getting Paul was considered by a contemporary writer "the crowning stroke of genius."[7] DuBose Heyward, author of *Porgy*, was commissioned to adapt the script, Dudley Murphy was named as director, and J. Rosamund Johnson engaged as musical director. Heyward actually wrote almost an entire new play, in which Jones's arrival in Haiti is preceded by events only alluded to in O'Neill's original work.

Jones was filmed twenty minutes from 42nd Street and Broadway at the old Paramount studios in Astoria, Long Island. Veteran William DeMille supervised the production, and most of the shots were staged inside. Krimsky considered going to Haiti for the jungle shots, but Paul, already sweltering in the heat, joked, "Bring in the trees right here; if this June weather holds out we've got plenty of tropic atmosphere right in the studio." But one location was, of course, prohibited. Paul's contract stipulated that he would not have to go south. When he was kept waiting for lights and cameras, he went to his room and rested or with Essie's help quietly rehearsed his part.

The film opened in September 1933 at the Rivoli Theater downtown and simultaneously at the Roosevelt Theater in Harlem, where during the first week of its run, blacks lined up and bought tickets to the tune of $10,000. Black heroes were rare enough in the movies, and when Jones snarled, "Maybe I killed one man in the States and maybe I'll kill another right now," the Harlem audience identified vicariously with his braggadocio, guffawing loudly.

Critical response to the film was divided, although Paul's acting was highly praised. The black press, at first favorable, found upon reflection, that the film was far from perfect because it perpetrated a stereotype. "Harlem dislikes 'Nigger,'" headlined the *New York Amsterdam News*. A white commentator, the Reverend James M. Gillis, editor of the influential *Catholic World*, objected to the celluloid

Paul Robeson in the movie version of *The Emperor Jones*. Reprinted with the permission of Joanna T. Steichen.

stereotype of the black man as "essentially craven." Gillis felt that the film reinforced society's false image of blacks and that blacks could not afford to take a detached view of their art. Three years later, a conference of Marcus Garvey's United Negro Improvement Association, held in Canada, would condemn *Emperor Jones* as part of "an international conspiracy to disparage and crush the aspirations of Negroes toward higher culture and civilization and to impress upon them their inferiority."[8]

Although Paul would later come to regret the film, he saw it at first chiefly as a work of art. Back in England, after shooting *Emperor Jones*, he found hope in the fact that it had not been made in Hollywood, and he expressed enthusiasm for Dudley Murphy's direction. According to the interview Paul gave to Doris Mackie in *Film Weekly*, he considered Dudley a man with an amazing insight into the true character of the Negro. "It is quite likely that the film will not sell in the Southern States of America," Paul told the British reviewer. "We had the British and Colonial markets in mind. . . . Over here you are quite prepared to acknowledge that the colored man is a human being."[9] The aspects that some blacks found offensive apparently eluded him. Was he out of touch with the day-to-day problems and sensitivities of American blacks? Or perhaps he let these take second place to other considerations. He later admitted that in those years, like most Negro performers, he was so glad for the opportunity to get a starring role that the content and form of a play or film was of little importance and he often failed to consider the feelings of blacks in general.

Paul arrived back in London on August 3, 1933, leaving behind him the highly controversial *Scottsboro* case, which had dominated talk in America. Nine black Alabama youths had been accused in March 1931 of raping two white girls aboard a freight train and were quickly convicted and sentenced to death. In a power play to head the defense of the youths the Communist International Labor Defense, headed by Paul's friend, William L. Patterson, had won out over the NAACP. The atmosphere surrounding the case was undoubtedly on his mind when, the day after Paul's arrival, *The Daily Express* ran an article by its film correspondent, quoting Paul as saying "the modern American is the lowest form of civilization in the world today." He was not much worried about counteracting white Americans' prejudice, according to remarks he made to the interviewer. What troubled him was the thought that if American blacks succeeded in being "exactly like the white man," they would destroy themselves within the next generation. "I want to lead the Negro out of this new Egypt into a new promised land," he said. A month later, when an interviewer asked Paul whether his attack on white Americans had been reported accurately, his comment was, "a trifle exaggerated." But according to the interview, which was published in *Film Quarterly*, he was still concerned about the tendency of blacks to model themselves on the white man.

Behind these and other views that would shift and change with time was Paul's continuing search to give his life a meaning and direction that could no longer be satisfied by fame, riches, and adulation. He and Essie were still frequent guests at Mayfair parties, but they were becoming increasingly ill at ease there. One day when Paul heard someone sharply rebuke his chauffeur, he thought to himself that it was no different from the way an American southerner would speak to a black man. His situation in well-to-do circles was becoming painfully clear to him, as he became aware of subtle and not too subtle prejudice of people like Evelyn Waugh, who in *Decline and Fall* would characterize him as immaculately turned out in formal attire, enervated, haughty in manner, with Regency *patois* driveling from heavy purple lips.[10] And he undoubtedly heard of the scandal Nancy Cunard had caused by inviting both blacks and whites to a private dance.[11]

By the beginning of 1934 Paul was busy studying Hebrew and Hebrew music. This was another expression of his deeper immersion in political and social issues. Expressing the close affinity he saw between blacks and Jews, he told a reporter for the *Glasgow Evening Citizen* that the persecution in Germany was "the most retrograde step the world has seen for centuries." Paul considered the Negro problem, according to the article, of much less importance to the world than the persecution of the Jews by the Nazis. He had autographed a number of copies for sale of an article he had written for a new Jewish weekly, the Glasgow paper reported, and he hoped to give a recital of Hebrew folk songs shortly.[12]

At the same time in his concerts in 1934 and after, Paul reduced the number of spirituals and American Negro folk songs in his programs, and included instead more and more Russian, Hebrew, and Irish songs. This in no way diminished his popularity among Africans who heard him. After a concert in Dublin in 1934, Larry Brown noticed that the five blacks who crowded around Paul looked at him adoringly, as though he were Moses. Paul's blackness, presence, and remarkable gifts all combined to make him appear a leader in the eyes of these young men, Brown thought. Later, when Brown asked him what he thought of becoming a Negro leader, Paul said he had never considered it and didn't think he had any desire to be. "Still, I'm sure this incident did have an effect on Paul," Brown remarked to Marie Seton.[13]

Africans in the British Isles had long considered Paul a hero. He had become especially friendly with the young people of the West African Students Union, which, from its beginning in 1925, had announced as one of its aims the restoration of sovereignty, lawfully and con-stitutionally, to native African rulers. WASU's members were considered agitators, but Paul was a frequent visitor to Aggrey House, their center at 47 Doughty Street. He participated in their activities and avidly listened to the unusually articulate group of students talk freely about the cultures of Africa. He felt a pride in Africa that grew "with the learning" and compelled him to speak out against the "scorners," he wrote later.

He also began taking courses at London University's School of Oriental Studies, which, with the aid of a Rockefeller grant in 1932, now offered courses in African languages and recruited Africans living in London to help. "Haphazardly," as he put it, Paul studied East Coast and West Coast languages. Swahili, he found to be flexible and subtle enough to convey Confucius's teaching, and he planned to make a comparative study of Asiatic, African, and Indo-European language groups. "If the people knew how closely they were related . . . in speech, song and expression, the world would be happier," he said.

Essie, too, was turning to African studies. For some time she had been haunting the British Museum and the libraries of the House of Commons, London University, and the London School of Economics. She began studying anthropology at the London School of Economics with Bronislaw Malinowski and Firth and at London University with William Perry and Hocart. Within a year she felt well enough informed to challenge what she felt were incorrect interpretations of the African mind and character, though her teachers and white classmates would insist that she was a "European" and did not understand the "primitive" mind. This infuriated her. She and Paul began to seek out Africans from all walks of life on their travels, and the more they talked with them, the more convinced they became that they were at heart the same people. They came to realize, Essie wrote later, that the

Negro problem concerned not only the 13 million Negroes in America, but also the 150 million Negroes in Africa and the 10 million in the West Indies.[14]

African culture, which blacks around the globe shared, was related to Arabic, Chinese, and Jewish culture, Paul wrote in an article published in March 1934 by the *Journal of Living and Learning*. His task, as he now saw it, was to arouse black awareness to this heritage which "could introduce a fresh spiritual and humanistic principle" to the world. In the same month Essie, on Paul's behalf, declined an invitation from Harold Moody, the Jamaican physician who had founded the League of Coloured Peoples, because, in her words, she and Paul felt that the Negroes who decided to remain in England "are of no importance whatever, in comparison to the major problem" of the 150 million of them in Africa.

A great opportunity to bring African culture to the eyes of Europe and America, Paul thought, would be the film he was scheduled to begin in the fall of 1934. Originally called *Bosambo* but retitled *Sanders of the River*, it was based on the adventure stories of Edgar Wallace, who as a young reporter had accompanied British colonialists to Africa. Wallace had intended to produce the Sanders stories himself, with Charles Laughton in the comic role of the African chief. But Alexander Korda, a Hungarian who had arrived in England in 1930, and whose productions included *The Scarlet Pimpernel* and *The Private Life of Henry VIII*, had always admired British colonial rule and wanted to do the film. He selected Paul, whose Bosambo was essentially serious, and cast American Nina Mae McKinney as Paul's sensuous wife. Korda also sent a fifteen-man camera crew to central Africa, where after four months and a total of 15,000 miles, they took 60,000 feet of film, some of which contained valuable shots of Africans in war, ceremonial, and fertility dances. Paul and Nina used some of the film as instruction in the dances, though only 2,000 feet were ultimately used.

Production of the studio film took place at the Shepperton Studios on the Thames in the fall of 1934. Over two hundred African and West Indian seamen, dockworkers, students—almost anyone with black skin, including Johnstone (later Jomo) Kenyatta—were recruited from the waterfronts of Cardiff, Glasgow, Liverpool, and London to appear in crowd scenes.

To Paul the experience provided further evidence of his identity with Africa. He and Pauli, who visited him on the set, were thrilled at the contact with so many black people. One day to his astonishment, he discovered that he could understand some of what two Ibo extras were saying to each other in their own dialect. One phrase he got was "aw bong." "Suddenly its reminiscence occurred to me—'Ol' Boy'—the musical phrase of the Spiritual . . ."15 While filming *Sanders* Paul also became more closely acquainted with Kenyatta, to whom he gave records and a record player. He and Kenyatta visited each other's homes, and the student from Kenya undoubtedly talked about the plight of his people there and his experience in Russia in 1929 and 1932. Kenyatta was struck by the similarity between the life of the Asiatic tribes he had seen in Soviet Central Asia and the life of his own people in East Africa. The changes that he would later bring as head of the Kenya government were foreshadowed as he wondered aloud to Paul what would happen to the tribes in Kenya under a new regime.

Whether or not he was aware of it before, Paul's contacts with the Africans on the set probably gave him a deeper understanding of the racism they suffered in England. In December, in an apparent change of mind, he did address the League of Coloured Peoples, telling them, "I am unquestionably leaving this country." Another article quoted him as saying, "In England I have found perfect freedom and peace. But my friends are not free. I pass through the doors of a hotel and they are stopped." After raising other blacks to a greater pride in African culture, he wanted to go to Africa some day to live among his people, he declared. "Among white men I am always lonely."

But by the end of December, when Paul and Essie embarked on a trip, it was not to Africa, but to Russia.

VIII:
Russia --"For the
First Time..."

On a day in late December 1934 Paul sat in the compartment he shared with Essie and their friend Marie Seton, staring silently as the Russian plain swept by, its monotonous expanse of snow relieved only now and then by birches standing alone or huddled in groves. The two women felt chilled from the cold north wind even though the compartment was heated. But Paul, who had hardly said a word all day, felt numb less from the cold than from what had happened in Berlin the day before.[1]

During his first visit to Germany in 1930 there had been some talk of Hitler, but most of the people Paul had met considered the little Austrian a fanatic not to be taken seriously. Paul knew that since then Hitler had taken over the country, but he had not expected what had occurred. On arriving in Berlin the Robesons and Marie had decided to walk the short distance to the hotel where they would wait for the evening train to the East. The streets were filled with people, and Paul noticed quick, furtive looks as he and the two women strolled along. A giant of a black man was not a common sight on the streets of Berlin, but neither wonder nor admiration were in the eyes that quickly looked at him and turned away. What at first Paul only sensed became clear as a group of brown-shirted Nazis standing around in their jackboots turned upon him, eyes filled with hatred. One or two brownshirts even propositioned him. Paul arrived at the hotel with the two women so shaken that he didn't want to leave his room, even to eat. Throwing himself down on the bed, he lay staring at the ceiling while Essie telephoned someone Paul had met and liked in 1930. The man, who was Jewish, came to the hotel immediately, and he soon was relating the horrors of the concentration camps where thousands of Jews and communists were being held. Suddenly, he stopped and said that he preferred to walk in the streets while he talked. Paul did not want to leave the room, so Essie and Marie accompanied him.

When they returned to the hotel room, they found Paul brooding angrily by a window. Later, he told Marie that he thought she and Kuh had been exaggerating when they told him about Germany. But his Jewish friend's obvious terror was unmistakable. "You know what this racism means in my case?" he asked. He and the two women decided they should eat in their hotel and they spent the afternoon in a cinema just down the street, where they watched a long African travelog presented by Kermit Roosevelt and his wife.

That evening at the station, Essie had gone off to see about the luggage while Paul and Marie went to locate the train. It had not yet come in, and the two had stood talking on the platform, which was nearly deserted except for a few scattered storm troopers. Suddenly Paul tensed and told Marie to continue talking as if she hadn't noticed anything. The storm troopers were forming a line, shoulder to shoulder, to Paul's left, and they stood between him and Marie and the passengers gathering on the platform. Apparently, a woman who thought that Marie was German had gone over to the storm troopers and complained about the disgraceful sight of a black man talking to a German woman. The storm troopers first stared, then began cursing and hurling epithets. Paul urged Marie to leave the platform. "There's time for you to get out," he said. But Marie edged closer to him, enraging the storm troopers even more.

As the name-calling increased, Paul became both fearful and angry. "It's how a lynching begins. If either of us moves, or shows fear, they'll go further. We must keep our heads." When Essie strode up, a second line of troopers formed behind her, and Paul and the two women found themselves hemmed in by a semicircle of shouting storm troopers. Paul figured that he could either allow them to rough him up in the hope that the women would be spared, or he could fight. He towered above the tallest of the men, and he could probably throw two or three onto the tracks and hurt several others if they made a move. Just when he decided to fight, he heard the train approaching in the distance.

"Get on!" he ordered. He quickly herded the two women aboard and climbed on himself, without waiting for their luggage, which arrived while the train was standing in the station.

It was only hours later, when they had crossed the German border into Poland, that Paul had been able to relax. "I never understood what fascism was before," he said. "I'll fight it wherever I find it from now on."[2]

When Paul and his party arrived at Negoroel, the Soviet customs station, a passport irregularity threatened to hold them up, but as soon as the officials discovered who Paul was they gave him a warm welcome and asked to hear the records he had brought along. Then without another thought for the passport problem, Paul, Essie, and Marie were allowed to board the train for Moscow.

Paul had wanted to go to Russia for some time, but the main purpose of this trip was to meet and confer with Sergei Eisenstein, the Soviet film director who had risen to fame in the 1920s with *Potemkin* and *Ten Days that Shook the World*. Marie Seton had long wanted Paul and her dear friend Eisenstein to meet because, as she once wrote Paul from Moscow, "you both have a thousand interests beyond your immediate work." When it was settled that the Robesons were coming, Eisenstein wrote Paul that he was looking forward to the "opportunity to talk (at last!) and we will see if finally we will get to do something together."

At the station in Moscow Paul and his party found Eisenstein at the head of a welcoming committee that included, among others, the black American actor Wayland Rudd. Rudd had come to Moscow in 1932, as one of two seasoned actors among twenty-two other American blacks who had been invited to act in *Black and White,* a Russian-sponsored film about black workers in Birmingham, Alabama. When poet Langston Hughes, a member of the group, read the script, he found its outline, in which racial discrimination and the capitalist system in the United States were denounced, plausible but its details "improbable to the point of ludicrousness." Yet his comment to officials that the script was not true to American life was met by "But it's been approved by the Comintern."[3] Hughes eventually persuaded the officials to keep the work songs and spirituals, get a new scenario, and import a German named Karl Yunghams, who spoke neither Russian nor English, as director. The film was finally abandoned, provoking the reaction expressed by Homer Smith, who later contended that the project had been given up because diplomatic recognition by the United States enjoined Russia from criticizing American internal policies.[4] Most of the blacks, who despite the fluctuations in official policy had been lionized at social and cultural gatherings, went home in outrage, but Wayland Rudd remained permanently in Russia, where he found work as an actor.

During Paul's two-week stay in Russia, Eisenstein was his constant companion. Many nights they talked until dawn about the evolution of languages, covering everything from the aboriginal tongues of Australia to the dialects of Africa and China. Seated in the filmmaker's cell-like room, Robeson played the African and Siamese recordings he had brought as presents to Sergei, and talked about the rhythms of African, Chinese, Thai songs and Negro spirituals. Eisenstein told Paul about his ideas for a new film *Black Majesty*. He wanted to use Paul and had already worked out his role in his mind. Paul was impressed.

He was even more impressed by the lack of racial prejudice he found in the Soviet Union. Children embraced him, showered him with affectionate names, and Russians everywhere accepted him "as a human being." It was quite a contrast to Berlin.

While in Moscow Paul was visited by Jack and Si-lan Chen, the children of Eugene Chen, the first Foreign Minister of the Chinese Republic. Jack, a writer, had married a Canadian girl, while Si-lan, a dancer, was married to Eisenstein's American student, Jay Leyda. To Paul, the couples seemed the embodiment of the cultures in which he was now interested. When they left, Paul paced the room. "Chen's the fulfillment of the Negro and Chinese culture when it's blended," he said. "You know, I'm an African. I feel it so strongly that, if necessary, I will die for Africa, but what should Africans care about American Negroes when most of them are Americans in culture? Can one expect a Chinese in China to be as concerned about the Chinese in San Francisco as about his own neighbors?"[5]

Paul met another black American expatriate, George Tynes, who had been born in Roanoke, Va., had originally gone to Russia in 1931 at the age of twenty-five on a two-year contract as an agricultural specialist and was put to work in the middle Asian Republic of Uzbekistan. "They thought I was a Uzbek," he said cheerfully a half-century later. He found Paul very candid and outgoing and recalled Paul's visit to a "special club for Americans. He was very happy, singing and joyful, telling about his football days, talking to everyone in pretty good Russian. He could win people over so much to his side so much . . . with his wisdom."

In the afternoon of Christmas Eve Eisenstein took Paul, Essie, and Britisher Albert Coates, who was conducting a series of concerts in Russia, to a Christmas dinner given by the Foreign Minister, Maxim Litvinov and his English wife, Ivy. After downing a feast of turkey, caviar, and vodka, the party danced wildly and happily—improvising everything from Litvinov's version of an Irish jig to Paul's Savoy Ballroom intricacies. Afterward Paul accompanied Eisenstein back to the director's apartment, where he sang some of *Boris Godunov*, which he had been studying.

At the end of a long day, Paul visited his old friend from New York, William L. Patterson, who had returned to Moscow for tuberculosis treatment. He and Patterson talked about the *Scottsboro* case, and Patterson told Paul that black liberation would require "immense sacrifice." He advised Paul to return to the United States and take part "in the great fight." Paul was not interested, but a few days later he said to a Russian journalist: "Our freedom is going to cost so many lives that we mustn't talk about the Scottsboro case as one of sacrifice. When we talk of freedom, we don't discuss lives. Before the Negro is free there will be many Scottsboros. The Communist emphasis in that case is right."[6]

Judging from this statement Robeson was clearly becoming more familiar with leftist ideas and analysis. But he was also responding to differences he felt personally and emotionally. He knew that in England he was treated like a visiting dignitary, while ordinary West Indians or blacks were often refused admission to public places. Russia, though, seemed not to make that distinction. The country gave him the feeling that he was "not a Negro but a human being. Before I came I could hardly believe that such a thing could be. In a few days I've straightened myself out. Here, for the first time in my life I walk in full human dignity. You cannot imagine what that means to me as a Negro."

What Paul saw and heard in Russia convinced him that the Soviets were ready to deal with the colored peoples of the world on a basis of equality. He was impressed with how "formerly oppressed nations were leaping ahead from tribalism to modern industrial economy, from illiteracy to the heights of knowledge," he wrote later. Education and the arts *were* thriving, he pointed out. If the Soviets could do this in two decades, why would it take Africans the 1,000 years to qualify for self-rule that colonialists insisted was necessary? The Soviet experiences in this regard could be applied by other peoples, Paul thought. American blacks would have a greater stimulus to recognize and embrace their heritage if Africans caught up with the modern world. The Russian experiences, it seemed to Paul, could be a potent aid in convincing "my poor people that their culture traces back to . . . great civilizations."

Essie, according to some reports, was less enthusiastic about Russia. It was clear to her, too, that Paul's reactions, coupled with his world renown, were potentially explosive. Paul's approval of communist principles might influence darker people all over the world. He might even become an issue in the only recently established U.S.-Soviet relations. Certainly, the point would not be lost on British imperialists.

Paul probably listened to Essie's concerns, but he could not turn his back on the profound new experience the trip to Russia represented. For years he had heard what people had told him about the country but could not believe it would be any different for him—with his black skin—than any other place. Obviously experiencing it himself changed that disbelief. He felt so intensely about what he saw and how he was received that when it was time to go home in January, he told reporters that he hoped every year to return to Russia once, and that he would spend less time in England and America.

Leaving Moscow in January 1935, Paul reiterated his intention to play Toussaint L'Ouverture in *Black Majesty* to be directed by Eisenstein, who appreciated Robeson most not as a black man but as a man who "was like himself a raceless and classless member of that section of humanity who looked forward to a society based on equal opportunity for all."[7] But it was as a black man that Paul poured out his deepest emotions to the diminutive Eisenstein before he left. "Maybe you'll understand," he said. "I feel like a human being for the first time since I grew up."

IX:
Birth of a
Political Artist

A social affair to which "all the world is going" is how *Harper's Bazaar* announced the premiere of *Sanders of the River*. Stars and celebrities from America and the Continent filled London's chic hotels for the benefit opening on April 3. Giant arc lights illuminated the patrons entering the Leicester Square Theatre, and dozens of bobbies held back onlookers. As an opening attraction the management showed the European premiere of *Band Concert*, the first color Mickey Mouse cartoon. Then followed what everyone was there for, Paul Robeson's new film.

Sanders of the River featured Sanders, whose code as district commissioner was: "You trusted all natives up to the same point, as you trust children . . . but the browny men of the Gold Coast, who talked English, wore European clothing, and called one another "Mr." were Sanders' pet abomination." Sanders represented "the British colonial approach at its frankest," writes Jeremy Murray-Brown.[1] He was "the perfect British D.C.," ruling with quiet authority, praised and feared by the natives. Bosambo, played by Paul, is an escaped, reformed convict from Liberia, representing "the best qualities of tribal Africa in popular imagination," according to Murray-Brown. Elected king of a tribe to which he brings some social reforms, Bosambo's position depends on the good will of Sanders, whose life he saves. The relationship between the two is always one of dependency, and the dialogue reflects this. When at one point Sanders returns to England for a brief vacation, Bosambo says, "Lord Sandy, it fills our years with sorrow to see you go away from us." To which Sanders replies, "Thank you, Bosambo. And in my place the Lord Ferguson will stay here and give the law to all the peoples of the River. I want you to obey him as if you were his own children."

To Paul, the message was not quite that benign. He sat seething in the audience, watching himself "smirking and indolent, a puppet on a string." Instead of the African culture he had wanted to bring to the eyes of Europe and America, there were "shots of grotesque and painted natives." When the film was over and he was asked to come up and speak, he reportedly walked out of the theater.

Reviewers and critics, for the most part, were favorably disposed toward the film and its stars and took due note of its propaganda, like the ads that promised the tale of "one white man who held the destiny of a native empire in the hollow of his hand. . . ."[2] Paul was singled out for praise; his physique, acting, and singing stole the show, one writer said. But he must have felt acute discomfort at another's comment that one of the frank and delicious moments of the film was at the point when an African chief asks Robeson, "Whose dog are you?" Young African nationalists called the film degrading to blacks and assailed Paul for being a white man's nigger. And Nancy Cunard, ever outspoken and shocking on racial matters, called it "pure Nordic bunk."

Why would Paul play the role of a cringing chieftain who sold out to British imperialism? A Capetown paper claimed that he had been trapped into playing the role and that the ending had been changed from the one originally shown to him. Some of the British actors who worked with him said Paul ended up playing the shameless Uncle Tom role because he was "too nice a guy" to assert his will during the filming. Then, when the film was finished, he was helpless; his contract gave him no control over the finished product. William N. Jones, a black American newspaper editor who returned from the Soviet Union a few months after the Robesons, wrote that according to sources in Moscow, Essie persuaded Paul to do the film. Certain British film-makers were anxious to talk about additional movies, Jones reported, to soften the impact that Paul's embryonic politics could have on blacks throughout the world.

Paul's own varying explanations during the year that followed the film's release did not clear up the situation. Evidently, he privately felt miserable about the movie, yet he told the *New York Amsterdam News* in October 1935: "To expect the Negro artist to reject every role with which he is not ideologically in agreement, is to expect him under our present scheme of things to give up his work entirely—unless of course he is to confine himself solely to the left theater." Later Robeson said that he agreed to take the role of Bosambo in order to portray African customs and culture, but while he was in Russia the film had been cut in such a way that it became something entirely different. Even after shooting retakes, on his return to London in January, he discovered that the director had squeezed in scenes to glorify colonial rule in the finished film, he said.[3]

By May 1936 Paul passed to a defensive stance. The attacks against him because of the picture were "correct," he told Ben Davis, Jr., who was later to become a dear friend. He had committed a *faux pas* which, "when reviewed in retrospect, convinced me that I had failed to weigh the problems of 150,000,000 native Africans . . . I did it all in the name of art . . . I hate the picture."[4]

Even as the controversy over *Sanders* continued, Paul began an intensive study of Marxism and Russia. He read and talked with people who had studied the Soviet system, people like Kingsley Martin of the *New Statesman* and *Nation;* Maurice Hindus, who had studied the Russian peasants; Andrew Rothstein, one of England's leading authorities on Marxist theory and Soviet economics. He also knew George Padmore, a Trinidadian and ex-Comintern agent who later became known as the "father of African emancipation." Padmore was living permanently in London after resigning from the Communist International on the grounds that Russia had sacrificed the liberation movements in Africa and Asia for better relations with the West. Paul's discussions with these people went on for six months; and at the end of this period, as he began to express his opinion, he was drawing closer to active socialists in various fields. But it was through the theater that he reflected his political ideology and race pride most vividly.

In the spring of 1935 he took the title role in *Basalik,* a play about an African chief who suspects the British colonial governor of planning to give concessions on the natives' land. Basalik poses as a servant, then abducts the governor's wife to prevent the plot. Margaret Webster played the "gossipy wife of a second in command," and ran away with the play, according to one critic. Paul's role was thin, but at least he felt he had played an African of dignity and honor, offsetting some of the humiliation he felt about *Sanders.*

A month later Paul opened in *Stevedore.* The American drama had been produced a year earlier in New York by the Theater Union, a labor group that was staging plays with working-class content at inexpensive prices. Originally entitled *Wharf Nigger* by its playwright Paul Peters, it had turned out so unactable that Peters and George Sklar completely rewrote it. As *Stevedore*, it became, according to Brooks Atkinson's *New York Times* review of the American production, "a swift and exciting drama of a race riot seasoned with class propaganda and presenting the American Federation of Labor as the Negro's best friend." Remarking that most people who go to the theater are "playgoers first and social philosophers at second hand," Atkinson's review said that what was most memorable were the "sprawling, humorous, frightened scenes of Negro life." The authors of *Stevedore*, he concluded, "have not forgotten that Negroes are human beings. They have produced a propaganda play in which you can recognize the natural exuberance of living people."

Marie Seton had read the reviews and passed them on to Paul, who thought it would be a good play to do in London with Ronald Adam and André van Gyseghem at the Embassy Theatre. "One of Robeson's high ideals was to found a theater for the expression of Negro dramatic art, and we all hoped that this play might be the beginning of it," Adam recalled.[5] Van Gyseghem, who was then studying Soviet theater in Moscow, returned especially to produce the play, with Paul taking the role of Lonnie Thompson, a black worker who is framed, arrested, and killed for his attempt to organize stevedores into an integrated union. Getting other black actors was something of a problem; African and West Indian students were recruited and both Larry Brown and John Payne, the black baritone, had roles.

The reviews were not particularly favorable. The play, wrote Ronald Adam, "turned out to be too propagandist . . . and was not the success anticipated."[6] For Paul, however, this was outweighed by the opportunity to have portrayed an ordinary Negro in everyday life.

During the spring and summer of 1935, world attention turned to the Italian ventures in Africa. Mussolini was preparing to extend Italy's African Empire to Ethiopia, partly in revenge for the Italian rout at Adowa in 1896. In return, Haile Selassie, who had become Emperor of Ethiopia in 1930, was attempting to get the Soviet Union, the United States, and other major powers to intervene with economic sanctions or other measures. William Patterson recalled that Paul "was moved by the tack that Litvinov was taking on Ethiopia" and noted that this had to have "had an effect on his thinking." Maxim Litvinov, as the chief spokesman of the Soviet Union, at first seemed to provide the main opposition to the Italians, though as the war progressed the Soviets sold oil to them. The United States refused help to either side.

Meanwhile, on September 25, 1935, Paul and Essie left for the United States aboard the S.S. *Majestic*. Pauli, eight, and Mrs. Goode were already living in New York. Paul was to give concerts in Milwaukee and Seattle and then go to Hollywood where, on November 18, production of the film version of *Show Boat* would begin. Universal Films had bought the rights to Edna Ferber's novel and had made a silent film with "talkie" intervals, featuring "Stepin Fetchit" (Lincoln Perry) as Joe. When they decided to make a sound version, Universal hired Oscar Hammerstein II and Jerome Kern to do the screenplay. Hammerstein wanted Paul to repeat his stage success as Joe the Riverman, and though Paul was not very anxious to go to Hollywood, he did take the role.

The film, produced at a cost of $2 million, co-starred Donald Cook, Helen Morgan, and Irene Dunne; Paul and Hattie McDaniel played the comic servants, Joe and Queenie. Hammerstein and Kern's scenario laced the original story with new songs for Paul, including "Ah Still Suits Me," which was a defense of his laziness. The famous "Ol' Man River" was sung here against the choral background of "Niggers all work on de Mississippi. . . ." Paul hoped such appearances would strengthen his ability to bargain in future films.

Variety, along with most other newspapers, praised Paul's rendition of "Ol' Man River," but many blacks and the Negro and Jewish press were highly critical of the shabby, lazy, loyal character he played.

The blasts hit home, and after *Show Boat* Paul grew increasingly pessimistic about the prospects for depicting black characters honestly on the screen. Very briefly, he considered giving up films, but on his return to England in early January 1936, he decided to take a role in *The Song of Freedom*. Paul played John Zinga, an American black, and the last descendant of an African family of royal descent that had been sold into slavery by the Portuguese. The film was important, Robeson said, because it blended African and black American culture; it was "the first film to give a true picture of many aspects of the life of the colored man in the west . . . a real man." *Variety* predicted box office success for the movie, and *The Pittsburgh Courier* praised it as "a story of triumph," yet the feeling persisted that the film still failed to measure up to Paul's talent. At any rate, distributors did not buy it, and the movie was never widely seen.

In August 1936 Essie and Paul, Jr. returned to London after a three-month tour of Africa that took them from Capetown to Cairo and provided Essie with a great deal of anthropological data. She also kept an extensive journal, which she hoped one day to turn into a book. A few weeks later Paul started work on *King Solomon's Mines,* with Cedric Hardwicke. The film was heavily budgeted, and Paul's salary was £8,000. Hopefully, Paul was to exercise some control over the finished product. He wanted to ensure that his characterization of Umbopas was to be more than a "splendid savage," even being tutored in Efik to help prepare him for some of the lines of the white hunter's singing servant who turns out to be a king. But once again Paul was disappointed, and incidentally many critics shared his discouragement, although this time the problem seemed less in director Alexander Korda's colonialist views than in his treatment of Rider Haggard's novel.

Paul's intense film activity was not unnoticed by Americans who wanted to capitalize on his fame and influence. In 1936 John Hamilton, then national chairman of the Republican party, visited Paul in London with a proposal that he return to America and campaign among Negroes for Alfred E. Landon for President. In exchange, Paul would be able to write his own ticket for future Hollywood contracts. Paul refused.

Late 1936 found Paul on another trip to Russia, and on December 20 he announced from Moscow that he would send nine-year-old Pauli to school there. The boy should not be forced to contend with racial discrimination at his tender age, Robeson said, and he later left him at the Moscow Model School for two years, during which time he would live at the Metropole Hotel with Essie's mother. When asked about the rumors that he was going to become a Soviet citizen, however, Paul replied, "America is my country."

Between 1934 and 1936 Paul developed his philosophy of culture in an outstanding and provocative series of essays and newspaper interviews. As historian Sterling Stuckey pointed out in a 1971 article in *Freedomways* magazine, Paul always identified great emotional depth and spiritual intuition as major components in black American culture but believed that a deep-seated feeling of inferiority blocked blacks' awareness of their culture and drove them to obsessively imitating whites. The answer, Robeson stressed, was for blacks to go back to their African roots, and he set out to lay the foundations for this new awareness. Paul had to grapple with the distorted image of black African history; he studied traditions, folk songs, and folklore and became proficient in several West African languages. He also launched into a comparative study of Indo-European, African, and Asian language groups, eventually embracing more than twenty-five languages.

The culture of American blacks was substantially influenced by Africa, Paul concluded. Negroes were too fundamentally different— mentally and emotionally—to be more than a "spurious and uneasy imitation" of the white man.

This thinking is reflected in the several articles he wrote during 1935, including "Negroes—Don't Ape the Whites" in the *Daily Herald* and "I Want Negro Culture" in the *Daily News-Chronicle.*

Paul felt that American blacks were at a disadvantage because their greatest asset—an "immense emotional capacity"—was discounted in the West; he marveled that blacks had managed to protect their cultural "actualities and potentials" despite the hostile environment. The Negro must use Western technology, he said, but reject its values, for Western man had gained increased power of abstraction at the expense of creativity. Negroes should therefore cultivate the qualities in their culture that tie them to the East and to Africa, for, as Stuckey points out, Robeson stressed "the need for creative equilibrium between the spiritual and the material, between a life of *intuition and feeling* and one of *logical analysis.*" It was a conflict that had great meaning for him in his own life.

Paul also said that blacks could move closer to nationhood, with his help, and stimulate an international cultural transformation, that would lead to the "family of nations" that had to evolve if mankind was to survive. Thus, his aim was a world of striving for deep spiritual and cultural values that would transcend "national, racial, or religious boundaries." By the mid 1930s Paul had a well-developed Pan-African view. He believed the "African states will be free some day. It may come about through gradual withdrawal of European power or there may be a sudden overturn. Differences between sections of the continent would indicate the eventual formation of a federation of independent black states, rather than a single great Negro republic or empire," he was to tell a New York reporter in January 1936.

Paul had certain of these themes in mind in early 1936 when he accepted the lead in *Toussaint L'Ouverture* by a young Trinidadian playwright, C. L. R. James. The drama spanned the period of Toussaint's political genesis during the 1791 Haitian slave revolt and his rise to power, his captivity, and his death. "We became intimates for the five or six weeks of preparation for the play," said James fifty years later. "One night in Manchester Paul proposed that the play tour with me as Dessalines," but it was never produced beyond the two scheduled performances given by the Stage Society at the Westminster Theatre in March.

In early 1937 Paul starred in *Big Fella*, a film based on Claude McKay's novel *Banjo*. He took the title role of a black émigré in France and insisted that the dialogue portray him with strength of character, as a steady and trustworthy man who worked on the docks for a living. To avoid the derogatory connotations of "Sambo," Paul and Essie had the film retitled *Big Fella*. Lawrence Brown, in his first and only movie role, and James Hayter completed the trio of Marseilles stevedores. Even Essie had a small role.

Paul quickly followed *Big Fella* with another in February 1937. For that one, entitled *Jericho*, he got a chance to go to Egypt, where some of the scenes were shot. It was an important trip for Paul, who, at thirty-nine, set foot on African soil for the first time. Released in the United States as *Dark Sands*, the film focuses on an American soldier, Jericho Jackson, who remains in Africa after World War I. Despite the fact that in one scene Robeson rears back and sings "Mama's Little Baby Loves Shortnin' Bread," the Washington *Afro-American* felt Paul redeemed himself in *Dark Sands*. Bosley Crowther of the *New York Times* wrote that the less said about the film the better, and likened it to the posturing and masquerading of *The Sheik*.[7] The English press, too, was lukewarm toward the production.

When *Jericho* was released, Paul announced his retirement from commercial films. This latest part was the best role he'd ever had, he said, yet even there African stereotypes had been perpetuated by contrivance, melodrama, and artifice. It only capped a protracted unhappiness with the course of his film career, with his own roles, and with the general characterization of blacks on the screen. Robeson's English films were certainly a departure from the Hollywood stereotype but not enough to please him. "I thought I could do something for the Negro race on the films; show the truth about them—and about other people too," Paul told the *Daily Worker* in London in November 1937. "I used to do my part and go away feeling satisfied. Thought everything was O.K. Well, it wasn't." He had found out time and again that the industry was not prepared to let him express the life, hope, and aspirations of blacks. "Any Negro who achieves success automatically becomes a representative of his people, and as such bears an added responsibility," he told the *Daily News-Chronicle* that same month. A year later, he was to be even more bitter about his movie experiences: "Films make me into some cheap turn . . . you bet they will never let me play in a film in which a Negro is on top," he told the same newspaper.

Robeson's political thought, molded by his studies of Marxism and his trips to the Soviet Union, was taking him to an irrevocable position. Turning his back on his lucrative film career was a first step. Deciding to abandon his Celebrity Concert Tour in England because it reached an essentially middle-class audience, was the next. "An artist needs an audience that responds to what he feels and is trying to express," Paul said. To reach less affluent, working-class listeners, he started singing in large music halls and cinemas in the provinces, sometimes as often as three times a day, keeping the admission price low.

Among the blacks who came to see the Robesons in London in 1937 were William Patterson, their old friend, and Max Yergan, whom Essie had met on her trip to Africa a year earlier. Yergan, who was destined to have a long, close, and ultimately explosive association with the Robesons, had been an official of the Coloured YMCA in South Africa. Shortly after Essie's visit he resigned that post because he found it "too conservative" and "opposed to the forces of peace and brotherhood." He returned to New York by way of Moscow, where Patterson said he introduced him to Stalin and Molotov. Back in the States, Yergan became a member of the National Negro Congress, which more nationalist-minded critics later charged, trained a group of Negro intellectuals for communism in the late 1930s.[8]

Yergan also formed the International Committee on African Affairs, with himself as director, and in 1937 he was touring Europe seeking members. He enrolled Paul; Leonard Barnes, a member of the faculty of the University of Liverpool and writer on colonial matters; and René Maran, French West Indian author of the Prix Goncourt winner, *Batouala,* all of whom, with Yergan, came to be considered the "Progressives on the Committee." They joined such American members as Raymond Leslie Buell, the Harvard political scientist who had written about Africa, and Ralph J. Bunche, professor of political science at Howard University and a student of colonial rule. The group's aims included informing the public of African affairs, helping

educate Africans to assume leadership roles, and promoting development of co-ops in Africa to organize the people and simultaneously
provide a mechanism for Africans to control their own destinies.[9]

By 1937 the Spanish Civil War and the fight against Franco had
become a symbol for many people around the world. In England it was
a constant topic for Paul and his friends, who were later to consider
Spain "a dress rehearsal of World War II. . . ." In June, while Paul was
still in Moscow, he learned that a benefit concert for Basque Refugee
Children would be held that month at Albert Hall in London. He
wanted to send a recorded message and recital from Russia but was
told that broadcasts were not permitted in the hall, so he hurriedly
returned in time to perform in person. Then he stated his position
before the gathering: "Every artist, every scientist, must decide now
where he stands. He has no alternative. There is no standing above the
conflict on Olympian heights. There are no impartial observers. . . .
The artist must elect to fight for Freedom or for Slavery. I have made
my choice. I had no alternative."

At Christmastime he sang at a rally to raise money for the Spanish
Loyalists, during which Labour party leader Clement Attlee talked
about his trip to the front lines and about the International Brigade.
Paul sang "Ol' Man River," and for the first time he changed the lyrics
from "I'm tired of livin' and feared of dyin'" to "I must keep fightin'
until I'm dyin'." The 9,000 people attending the rally roared their approval, but when composer Oscar Hammerstein heard about it much
later, he was furious.

On January 16 Paul sang at a second rally and then left for Spain
himself. He arrived in Barcelona on January 23 and traveled by truck to
Madrid, where he sang before troops of the International Brigade and
in hospitals. Later, he traveled to other European cities as well, singing
and raising money for the Republican cause.

Spain was another turning point in Paul's life. There he saw the
working men and women who were fighting Franco and the largely
upper-class Falangists who wanted to continue exploiting the Spanish
workers and the colonies. In Barcelona he met Nicolas Guillén, the
black Cuban poet and journalist who had been fighting in Spain for
over seven months, and in Madrid he played street football with
neighborhood boys, while Italians and Germans shelled a nearby area.
He was deeply impressed by the spirit of the Spanish people and
carried away by Spanish folk music, much of which, he claimed, closely

resembled Negro music. It was for that reason too, he said, "I want to return to Spain when there is more calm—when the Republicans shall have won the war."

In response to what he saw, Paul's spirituals took on a new militance. When he sang "Strike the cold shackles from my leg," the audience sensed he was singing about Spain. And he enunciated this in a radio broadcast from Madrid: Under fascism he wouldn't have been permitted to develop his voice because of his race, he said on the air. He was proud of the International Brigade, he went on, with its black and white volunteers from America. He spoke of black men like Oliver Laws, Milton Herndon, Alonzo Watson, who left their homes and died in a foreign war zone. Whereas in the past, musicians, concert artists, and entertainers were the leading black ambassadors of the Negro in Europe, Robeson pointed out, at Valencia, Madrid, and Tarazona, the black men in Spain were not entertainers but fighters—volunteer fighters. Seeing them engendered a "new, warm feeling for my homeland . . . and I knew in my heart that I would surely return there some day."

After Spain, Paul returned to England and his regular concert career, but he expanded his political activity and became more involved with the British Labour movement. He felt "the heart of (anti-fascist action) was the forces of Labor—the trade unions, the cooperatives, the political parties of the Left—but other broad sections of the population were involved, including many from the middle class and people from the arts, sciences and professions."[10]

To find material suitable for his talent and compatible with his ideology, Paul turned to the leftist theater. He became a member of the advisory council of the Unity Theatre, a group that planned to put on plays with a working-class message. There was no star system, and many of the actors were trade union members who rehearsed at night after work. Thus, in June 1938 Robeson appeared in the Unity Theatre's production of *Plant in the Sun*, a short play by American writer Ben Bengal that was directed by Robeson's friend, Herbert Marshall. Portraying a sit-down strike and union-organizing in the United States, it was a prolabor play that barely escaped being pure propaganda, but most reviewers liked it.

The next summer the Robesons spent a great deal of time with Horace Cayton, the black co-author of *Black Metropolis*. On his first visit to Paul's home, Cayton found Paul "alone, wearing a dressing gown and studying Chinese with the aid of a language record." On another

Robeson entertaining Republican troops during the Spanish Civil War

A publicity photo for *Proud Valley*, 1939

occasion Paul and Essie took the Caytons, along with another friend, "an unbelievably beautiful Swedish-English woman named Essma Hutchins," to a night club. London was blacked out due to the war scare, and the doorman was about to turn the party away until he recognized Paul's face from the light of the door. Inside, the West Indian bandleader sent champagne, and the management and a party of Hollywood people whom Paul knew sent wine. In the cab going home, Cayton's wife "flirted outrageously with Paul to Essie's great discomfort" while Cayton concentrated on the beautiful Swedish girl.

Cayton, a disenchanted communist, recalled many political talks with Paul, who was anxious for news about America, he noted. Most of the Robesons' friends were Marxists, and one evening he was "attacked for what the group called my moderate, even reactionary point of view." After vain attempts to vindicate himself, Cayton said, "Their insufferable self-righteousness began to infuriate me." Only Essie's intervention kept the argument from becoming murderous. Cayton thought the Robesons' political views were not widely known in America.[11] Years later Poppy Cannon, who was to become Mrs. Walter White, recalled Walter's remarking after talking with Paul in New York on the "strange alteration" in his political views.[12]

In 1939, Paul finally found a film he could be proud of making. *Proud Valley* was based on an idea by Herbert Marshall, who helped to produce it for Michael Balcon's Ealing Studio, and Paul and the company traveled to the Rhondda Valley for the shooting in the summer of 1939. In a role meant to be a symbol of working-class solidarity Paul played a black coal miner who goes to Wales at the height of a coal depression and tutors and helps the miners. War restores prosperity, and Paul eventually gives his life for his fellow miners during a cave-in. The movie received mixed reviews, but the *Afro-American* thought that in theme and character it far surpassed anything Hollywood had produced in its treatment of blacks. But Paul's mind was light years away from the reviews.

During the filming of *Proud Valley,* Hitler had invaded Poland, and World War II had erupted. He and Essie had been thinking of returning to America for some time, particularly in the face of the Chamberlain government's relationship to Germany. Paul was to write later, ". . . the more I became part of the Labour Movement the more I came to realize that my home should be in America."

Paul felt he "must be among the Negro people" during the world crisis that clearly was ahead "and be part of their struggles. . . ." He planned to take to American blacks his well-defined Pan Africanist views and his attempt to "build a unity" between them and "their struggling kinfolk in the colonies. . . ."

On September 30, 1939, he and Essie stepped onto the boat that bore them to New York.

X:
Ballad for
Americans

What we have to say seriously can be simply said. It's this: Democracy is a good thing. It works. It may creak a bit, but it works. And in its working, it still turns out good times, good news, good people . . . Life, liberty and the pursuit of happiness—of these we sing!" It was a month after Paul returned to the United States that Burgess Meredith spoke these words on a CBS series called "Pursuit of Happiness" to introduce "The Ballad for Americans."

Originally titled "Ballad of Uncle Sam," the song had been written by John LaTouche and set to music by Earl Robinson as part of a play called *Sing for Your Supper*, one of the dramas that killed the Federal Theater Project of the 1930s because, according to Congressman J. Parnell Thomas, it was propaganda for "Communism and the New Deal." A young CBS producer named Norman Corwin fished the song out of the ruins. "Wouldn't Robeson knock the hell out of this?" he exclaimed when he saw it. He renamed the selection "The Ballad for Americans" and decided to use it to inaugurate the new series.

Paul, too, had been enthusiastic about the song. Its theme of black-white brotherhood appealed to him, and he saw described in it the democracy envisioned by Thomas Jefferson and Abraham Lincoln. For days he and Larry Brown had worked on it. "It was unlike any other cantata," Larry remarked. "As we worked, Paul impressed his personality on it. He breathed life on it."[1] Then Paul spent another five or six days with Earl Robinson, carefully adapting the key to his range.

His enthusiasm was due in part to a certain optimism about the

America to which he had returned. In the early 1930s, as Paul sprinted from inexperienced actor to stage and film star to concert idol to political artist in Europe, blacks in America had passed through a period of trials and uncertainty to a measure of hope. The "Great Migration" from the South during and following World War I had given blacks political leverage in northern and western cities. By the 1932 national election they abandoned the Republicans to whom they had clung since the Civil War and turned to the Democrats and their candidate, Franklin Delano Roosevelt. Two years later Arthur W. Mitchell of Chicago, a former Republican, became the first black Democrat elected to the House of Representatives. When in 1937 a railroad conductor forced him to leave a first-class car, Mitchell took his case to the highest court in the land and became the first black to argue his own case before the Supreme Court. He won. Meanwhile Roosevelt, and his wife Eleanor, were winning increasing acceptance among blacks as a result of their more liberal personal attitudes, the appointment of blacks to government positions, and their consultation of Negro advisers, known as the "Black Cabinet."

As the 1930s progressed, Roosevelt's New Deal, at first of little benefit to blacks, provided new opportunities, with federal projects such as the Farm Security Administration, the Public Works Administration, the Works Progress Administration, the Federal Writers Project, the Federal Theater Project, and the Civilian Conservation Corps. In 1937 A. Philip Randolph's Brotherhood of Sleeping Car Porters won a contract from the Pullman Company as a result of the passage of the Wagner Act, and a year later the CIO emerged as the first large-scale interracial industrial union.

In the arts there had been a momentous breakthrough. When the Daughters of the American Revolution had refused to let Marian Anderson sing in their Constitution Hall, Mrs. Roosevelt resigned in protest, and Secretary of Interior Harold Ickes invited Miss Anderson to sing outdoors at the Lincoln Memorial. On Easter Sunday 1939 she stepped forward on the platform of the Memorial before a vast unsegregated audience. "There seemed to be people as far as the eye could see," she recalled. "The crowd stretched around the reflecting pool onto the shaft of the Washington Monument. I have a feeling that a great wave of good will poured out from these people, almost engulfing me." After a program of classical songs and several spirituals, including "My Soul is Anchored in the Lord," she ended the program with "America." Racism and segregation were still very much

Paul and Essie Robeson, about 1938   Wide World Photos

alive, however. In July Paul was invited to tea in one of New York's
leading hotels and, upon approaching the front elevator, was told to
use the freight elevator. "Several years back I would have smarted at
this insult and carried the hurt for a long time. Now—no—I was just
amused and explained to the elevator boy . . . that I was the guest of
honor. . . ."

Back in the States for good, Paul and Essie settled into a Harlem
apartment at 555 Edgecomb Avenue that "was just opening up to
blacks." Their old friend, William L. Patterson, and Louise, his second
wife, lived farther down the block at 409 Edgecomb, which, after
Strivers Row, became the place where everybody lived—Walter
White, Thurgood Marshall, Roy Wilkins, among other notable blacks.
"Paul was in and out of our house as was everybody—Langston

Hughes, Jacques Romaine, the Haitian writer," Louise Patterson recalled thirty-five years later.

Pauli, now nearly twelve, became an American schoolboy when he was enrolled at the Ethical Culture School. Larry Brown also settled in Harlem and became close to William Patterson, who remembers him as a "very great guy" and a "humanist" with no political philosophy, who helped anyone he could.

Early in January 1940 Paul opened in *John Henry*, a musical drama with social overtones. Most reviewers found the play about the legendary black hero badly flawed, but they applauded Paul's return to the American stage. Brooks Atkinson of *The New York Times*, for example, found him larger than life. By the end of the month, however, it was not a performance, but a nonperformance that was drawing criticism from the press.

The Herbert Hoover Relief Fund announced a benefit for Finland and informed the press that Paul had refused to participate. Finland had been attacked by Russia in November of 1939 after refusing to allow installation of the bases the Soviet Union had been promised in the Russo-German Non-aggression Pact. But Paul declared that he was not sure the news reports of Russia's attack on Finland were true. He had had firsthand experience with press distortion, he said, and if the reports were accurate, Finland must have provoked the attack. The year before he had seen Russians fighting alongside American and other volunteers in the Spanish Civil War, and he found it hard to believe that the Russians were turning "fascist" themselves. "Robeson," wrote the Associated Press, "who has lived in England for the last ten years . . . whose son was educated in Moscow, said he was not personally a Communist. . . ."[2]

If Paul's stand on Finland was problematic, it was not apparent on his cross-country concert tour in late winter and spring, which, in the wake of "Ballad for Americans," was highly successful. Some 30,000 people jammed the Hollywood Bowl to hear him sing *The Ballad for Americans*, and he held in "rapt interest" the inmates of San Quentin prison when he sang for them. A few days later in Chicago a reported 160,000 gathered at Grant Park to hear him. A few reviewers noted signs of wear in his voice, but others found his voice unchanged. It was on this tour that Paul began to cup his hand behind his ear while he performed, a technique that allowed him to hear himself while he was singing and helped him project in large open areas.

Paul's refusal to sing before segregated audiences endeared him to blacks. "It is easy to understand why Paul Robeson is the most beloved and greatest of artists we have produced," the *Chicago Defender* wrote on August 3, 1940. "Robeson is an artist-fighter for Negro America. . . . He is of the people and for the people."

During this time he made several efforts to help other blacks break into the theater. He contributed money to the Harlem Suitcase Theater, sponsored by Langston Hughes and Hilary Phillips. The group produced Hughes's *Don't You Want To Be Free?* in a loft above Harlem's famous Frank's Restaurant, with Robert Earl Jones (James Earl Jones's father) in the leading role. Paul's contribution enabled the group to hire as full-time artistic director, Thomas Richardson, who brought in such actors as Owen Dodson and Canada Lee. In September Paul, pianist Hazel Scott, and Richard Wright appeared at a benefit for the Negro Playwrights Company, which attracted 5,000 people to the Golden Gate Ballroom in Harlem.

It was about this time that Paul began dropping in regularly at Café Society Downtown to hear an outstanding but insecure young singer named Lena Horne, who was just beginning her rise to fame. Paul had been an "adopted son" of her grandmother, Cora Calhoun Horne, who had been "like a mother to me when I needed a mother most." And Lena had "often peeped over the banister to get a glimpse of the tall, solemn, diffident young man" who visited their Brooklyn home. Now he asked, "Would you let me be your friend?" Lena, who had dropped out of high school, was hesitant, because "he was sure to think I was an ignoramus." Gradually, Paul helped her learn to respect herself and her profession, which she worried was considered déclassé. Paul and Lena dined together, talked together. "To my amazement, the stories he told in answer to my questions carried the same hurt, the same denial, the same rejection all our people suffer, . . . But . . . Paul wasn't at all bitter. . . . It was the way he looked at things. He could see everything that was good and fine and beautiful in America. He knew the firm foundation on which America was built. He knew the tradition of our great land; he knew so much about what our people have given America, and he believed with all his heart that some day the mighty dream of the founders of our nation would come true. He was deeply, deeply angry about what all our people suffer. But it was an understanding anger. Never, never was he angry against white people as a group."[3]

In the spring of 1940 the Nazi war machine swept through Denmark, Norway, the Netherlands, and Luxembourg; France fell in

June. The fighting in Europe brought out all the contradictions and divided loyalties fostered by discrimination against American blacks. They detested Nazi Germany, of course, and had long been in the forefront of Americans condemning Nazism and fascism. Soon after Hitler's rise to power in 1933, for example, black educator Kelly Miller had compared the persecution of the Jews to Klan attacks on blacks. And when the Nazis stepped up their anti-Jewish campaign in 1938, Congressman Arthur W. Mitchell requested President Roosevelt to "use every reasonable and peaceable means . . . in securing protection for the Jewish people. . . ." Nevertheless, at the time of the Blitzkrieg, many black Americans felt that this was not their war. Memories of the violent attacks against black soldiers on their return from Europe after World War I were still alive. It was difficult for blacks to become enthusiastic about democracy in Europe, when they had little of it at home.

Shortly after his return to America, Paul had said in an interview with the *New York Amsterdam News* that he felt the war was an attempt by Chamberlain and Daladier to uphold fascism, though not Hitler, and to save Germany for Western civilization, against her own leadership, not to achieve democratic ends. For these reasons, he said, he didn't think the United States, and blacks in particular, should be drawn into the conflict. These statements were hardly distinguishable from the official Communist party line, which with the conclusion of the Hitler-Stalin Pact in August 1939, had been trying to prevent the U.S. government from aiding the Allied Powers. In August 1940 Paul again spoke out against the war and American involvement in it.

Paul's politics were now beginning to have some effect on his career. One critic took him to task for his inclusion of labor songs, and a radio appearance was canceled. A New Jersey youth group even actively campaigned against him. Despite such controversies Paul's popularity and earning power continued to climb.

At this point Robeson's politically hardening line brought him into conflict with some liberal blacks who wanted to protest against racial injustices. In late 1940 A. Philip Randolph, concerned about continued discrimination against blacks in defense plants, had begun planning a protest demonstration. Local committees were set up in cities with large black populations, and in addition to pressuring for jobs in their communities, members were to participate in an actual "March on Washington" in late June 1941. After June 22—when Germany violated the Hitler-Stalin Pact of 1939 and invaded the Soviet Union, prompting widespread U.S. sympathy for Russians for the first time since 1917—government officials made strenuous efforts to prevent the march. They were worried about the effect of a massive Negro protest march as international war tensions heightened. President and Mrs. Roosevelt, Secretary of War Henry Stimson, Secretary of the Navy Frank Knox, and Mayor Fiorello La Guardia of New York all tried to dissuade Randolph. After several conferences President Roosevelt finally promised to issue an order "with teeth in it," if Randolph would call off the march. The President created the Committee on Fair Employment Practices as a result.

Paul's personal position on the demonstration is not known. But the procommunist left wing with which he associated, had, as late as May, attacked Randolph, Walter White, and others as "red-baiting social democrats" who "use the fight against Negro discrimination for a war which means continued misery and lynching under the capitalist system." This stance was part of a vigorous, antiwar campaign that extreme leftists had conducted, as they called on blacks to oppose American involvement in the European war. It was the special duty of the communists to show that it would be a mistake if blacks "demanded jobs in exchange for support of the war-making plans . . ." Max Yergan had written in the *Daily Worker* on May 24. The war, he said, would "usher in destruction of democratic rights and denial of the meager civil liberties he enjoys already."

After the German invasion of Russia Paul increased his overt political activities, which were no longer against military involvement. In July the militant National Maritime Union made him an honorary member. At its convention in Cleveland he sang ten songs and told the interracial union that fascism had "at last come to grips with the one power that will show it no quarter," meaning Russia. He urged America to give the Soviets all the aid it could. On September 29 he joined Max Yergan, Vito Marcantonio, Elizabeth Gurley Flynn, and others in speaking at a mass rally to free Earl Browder, the communist party leader who had been imprisoned reportedly because of his antiwar activities. (He was released in May 1942 by special presidential pardon and immediately resumed leadership of the party.) And in October during an interview in Milwaukee Paul said that he saw the war as a collision between conservative and liberal forces. "I think Russia will fight on, and on, and still on until somehow victory is won. . . ."

It was in 1941 that Essie stopped traveling with Paul on his tours and decided to live outside of New York. She wanted to write a book about the trip she and Paul, Jr., had made to Africa in 1936 and felt it would go more smoothly away from the bustle of Harlem. In Enfield, Connecticut, she found a house on the main road of the town, situated on two and a half acres with a beautiful view of hills and fields. Since the only blacks in the town were a single low-income family, Essie inquired about the possibility of any racial trouble if she and Paul bought "The Beeches." The bank reported that nobody would object, so the Robesons bought the house and put in a swimming pool, a tennis court, and a billiard room. An extra-long bed was installed in Paul's bedroom. Essie enrolled at Hartford Seminary to work for her doctorate in anthropology, and Paul, Jr., was sent to the Technical High School in Springfield, Massachusetts.

As for Paul, he had received many offers from Broadway and Hollywood since returning to America but he had found none of them acceptable. "This resentment in my people goes deep," he said in early 1941 about film characterizations of blacks. "I can't let them down by doing the things they hate." Eventually, however, he relented and reluctantly accepted a role in a Twentieth-Century Fox production, called *Tales of Manhattan*. Charles Boyer, Rita Hayworth, Ginger Rogers, Cesar Romero, Henry Fonda, Charles Laughton, and Edward G. Robinson starred in six vignettes that told the odyssey of a dress coat that finally falls onto the plot of land tilled by poor sharecroppers, played by Paul Robeson and Ethel Waters. The coat contains $43,000 stolen by its previous owner, and the money is divided among the poor of the community who shout and praise God for this unexpected windfall. "I wanted to pose the problem of the Negro sharecropper, but not in this way. (Producer Borris Morros) and I argued all through the film. Borris knows I wasn't satisfied."[4] Paul said he didn't blame Negroes who later picketed the film protesting its stereotyped, superstitious blacks and distortion of the black religious experience. Paul, in fact, joined in the picketing and after *Tales*, never acted in another commercial film, because producers didn't choose "to offer me worthy roles to play . . . I don't want to be a noble savage."

In the predawn hours of December 7, 1941, Japanese planes attacked the U.S. Naval Base at Pearl Harbor. A chunky young mess attendant crept through the crashing bombs, pulled his wounded superior to safety, and then shot down at least four Japanese Zeroes. Dorie Miller, a black man, became one of America's first heroes of World War II. Paul, like black Americans everywhere, was proud of Dorie Miller, but saddened that war had finally struck.

The Robeson family, at "The Beeches" in Enfield, Connecticut

Nevertheless, he was determined to do his share in the war effort. He criss-crossed the country giving recitals to various groups, often at no fee. He sang at ammunition plants and for such organizations as the Quebec Committee for Allied Victory, the Washington Committee for Aid to China, Russian War Relief, and the Navy Relief Special Events Committee. Three organizations claimed his special attention: the Committee to Aid China, for which he had given a benefit concert in spring 1941; the Joint Anti-Fascist Refugee Committee, which was aiding Spanish Loyalists, and the Council on African Affairs (formerly the International Committee on Africa), for which he had served as chairman since 1937.

His art itself became increasingly involved with social issues. In 1942 he recorded "King Joe," a blues number written by Richard Wright, glorifying Joe Louis and expressing Wright's concept of the blues as songs of struggle and revenge. The music was written by Count Basie and featured a trumpet introduction by Buck Clayton. John Hammond directed the recording, which sold well, with an advance order of 40,000 copies at thirty-five cents each. In the view of Wright biographer Michel Fabre, "Robeson's participation in the publicity campaign indicates that the Party considered the recording possible propaganda material."[5]

That same year Robeson was linked peripherally to a House Un-American Activities Committee investigation, when Native Land, a film for which he had done the commentary in 1940, was released. The movie's theme was "America's fight for freedom in our own times," and it was based on material taken from the findings of the La Follette-Thomas Senate Civil Liberties Committee in 1938, which reported brutal violations of the Bill of Rights. Nevertheless, according to Congressman Martin Dies, who headed HUAC, the Robert Marshall Foundation, which supposedly gave money to "allegedly Communist-front organizations," had subsidized Pioneer Films, producers of Native Land. Dies's committee also mistakenly claimed that the film was based on Richard Wright's Native Son.

Some of the press argued that Native Land should not have been released during wartime. But the New York Herald Tribune felt that war distribution of the movie would help make Americans "alert to combat subversive disruption of free speech at home" while fighting for these freedoms overseas. Using Robeson, it said, was "a stroke of genius."

XI:
The Moor

For years producers such as Lillian Baylis of London's Old Vic had corresponded with Paul about playing *Othello* in the United States. Paul and his friend actress-director Margaret Webster also talked repeatedly of this possibility, both in New York and in London, where he was sometimes invited to her home or to the home of her mother, actress May Whitty. But Webster recalled that it never materialized because producers feared race prejudice, were afraid to invest in it. "Everybody was scared. Most of them said that an American audience would never come to a theatre to see a black man play a love scene with a white woman."[1] Still she remained convinced that a production starring Paul would be a "landmark in the American theatre and in the history of American consciousness. . . ." She persisted until she finally got the backing to do the play in New England tryouts.

The announcement was made in the spring of 1942: Paul Robeson would appear in a production of *Othello* at the Brattle Theater in Cambridge, Massachusetts with Uta Hagen, a fine young actress, as Desdemona, and José Ferrer, a vibrant Puerto Rican married to Hagen, as Iago. Now famous enough to write his own ticket, Paul insisted on Margaret Webster as director.

Paul was quite frankly thrilled to be playing *Othello* again, and he was determined to triumph far beyond his 1930 performance. He re-evaluated his concept of the role, emphasizing what he felt was its deep social meaning for the present. He took the role apart, speech by speech, examining each word for its meaning. He sought out Shakespearean authorities and listened carefully to directors, but when their concept of the character conflicted with the way he felt a great Negro warrior would act, he played it his way. He employed the same technique from his earliest days in the theater—bringing to the role a thorough understanding of the script and its intent. "I am not a great actor like José Ferrer . . . All I do is feel the part. I make myself believe I am Othello, and I act as he would act," he said.

On August 10, 1942, the cast gave its first preview performance, at Brattle Hall in Cambridge, the first time in America that a black actor had played *Othello* with a white supporting cast. The day was hot and humid. All 400 seats were filled, and people lined the walls, as hundreds more were turned away at the box office. The stage was very small, and although he had lost 30 pounds for the role, with his bulk, Paul felt particularly nervous. Few tremors marred his commanding voice and dignified manner, however. Margaret Webster recalled the opening night: "The hottest I ever remember; the theatre had a corrugated iron roof, and was packed to the rafters with sweating humanity! We sweated too, whether from nerves or natural causes, or both; there was tension in the air. . . ."[2] For three hours the audience endured the sticky heat; they neither rattled chairs nor rustled programs. They hung attentively on his lines when Othello spoke before the Venetian ducal council, pleading that he won his wife fairly; they responded when he stepped into the drunken brawl that cost Cassio his commission.

When the final curtain dropped, the audience stamped their feet in a steady, swelling stomp, the traditional undergraduate salute. The Boston press was also enthusiastic. Within twenty-four hours, this excitement reached New York. Managers there kept the long-distance wires busy asking for a piece of the show, and *Variety* predicted the production would "hurl Broadway on its practically invulnerable ear."

The production moved next to a tryout in Princeton, where many of the "princes" from Paul's boyhood sat in the audience. Cousin Minnie Carraway, whose mocha visage bore the unmistakable signs of the Robeson ancestry, sat in the McCarter Theater for the first time in her life. "Oh, he was wonderful," she recalled thirty-three years later, as she sat a few blocks away from Paul's boyhood house on Green Street. While the production was in town, she remembered, she glanced up one day from her seat on the front porch swing to see Paul's huge figure approaching. "He came right here on the porch and sat down and we talked for an hour." Shakespearean scholar, Arthur Colby Sprague, who was also at the Princeton performance, remarked, "I was left at the close wondering whether his performance had not approached the greatness attributed to actors in other times."

Despite the initial excitement it took nearly four months for details of a New York production to be worked out. Neither Margaret

Webster nor Paul felt the show was ready for Broadway yet. Paul wanted to study the play further. He had always rejected the conventional interpretation of *Othello* as a man driven by jealousy. Rather, he felt that Othello was driven to murder his beloved wife because the Moor thought she was unfaithful to him and this alleged disloyalty had not only deeply hurt him but also threatened his honor. Paul felt Othello's rage "is maddening, he is out of his head: and I know what that is like because I felt it once myself," he recounted a couple of years later. "One time I went out of my head in a rage and night after night out there on the stage I remember it." He was referring to his tryout for the football team at Rutgers, when he had been badly beaten up.

In January 1943 the Theatre Guild announced that Paul would open in *Othello* at the Shubert Theater in New York in the fall. For a time it appeared that the original cast could not be assembled because José Ferrer was nearly drafted. In the end, however, Ferrer and Hagen were able to appear, and the original cast was together again. The play previewed at New Haven's Schubert Theater on September 18, moved on to Boston for a two-week run, and came down to Philadelphia in early October. Divided reviews—but most of them highly laudatory—accompanied every production. Now it was time to face the formidable New York theater world, with that city's first *Othello* in six years.

The audience on the evening of October 19, 1943, was more diverse than usual; the expensively dressed rubbed shoulders with house painters and college students. Actors, musicians, and artists sat beside European refugees and Harlem residents, as Paul brought the Moor to life. He was obviously different from other Othellos in race and culture; his manliness and humanity were the same. Certainly, he was capable of deeply touching the emotions of the spectators, for when the curtain fell, the spontaneous release of feelings spurted forth in loud applause. "Paul! Paul! Paul!" came the chorus of shouts washing over him. The clamor did not cease until he had taken ten curtain calls.

The critics filed out with the audience to return their verdicts. Most of them hailed the production as "terrific," "distinguished," a "consummate revival," "stirring." The dissenters commented on such things as Paul's voice—"a trifle monotonous"—and Stark Young felt Paul lacked the "ultimate requirement" for the role—"a fine tragic method."[3]

By and large, Paul was happy over the reviews. He was staying with his old friends Harold (Gig) and Bert McGhee when the play opened. (He and Essie were living more and more apart now. While there was

Othello, starring Paul Robeson in the title role and Uta Hagen as Desdemona. Margaret Webster, who directed the play, also took the part of Emilia.

no outward break they felt free to pursue their separate interests, and Paul's work kept him in New York or traveling much of the time. However, Essie still handled many of his multitudinous business dealings, and he visited Enfield fairly regularly.) The morning after opening night, Gig brought in all the newspapers. Paul started to beam as he read them. "Boy, I'm lucky," he said, his eyes smiling. "Did you ever know such luck as I have?"

It was as if Paul had made his first success, Gig McGhee said, and he never forgot that reaction. Modesty was a basic part of Paul's character according to McGhee. "If at times he acts as if he were not, it's circumstances compelling him to act in a way other than he really wishes to."[4]

Each exacting performance was a great emotional strain, and Paul seemed to work harder in one performance than in three concerts, where he routinely lost ten pounds. Yet Paul did not get bored with playing *Othello* every night. The challenge of doing Shakespeare, combined with his feeling that he was preparing the way for other black actors, kept the play fresh and alive for him. He believed he had convinced Shakespeare lovers that the "role definitely belongs to a Negro and the naturalness is lost when a white man does it under burnt cork."

The controversy over whether Shakespeare meant a black man to be Othello had continued. Margaret Webster was adamant that "black skin is more than a physical requirement . . . it implies a great many psychological requirements which the play needs, if it is to be understood. Othello was of a different race from Desdemona. That is what the play is about."[5]

The presentation of the problems of a black man was "right up my alley," Paul said before the play opened, and Shakespeare had provided a meatier, more realistic part, he felt, than any of the contemporary playwrights or filmwriters had managed.

That this was an exciting *Othello* is clear from the fact that it was much written about and that it drew capacity houses for so long, despite the mixed critical reaction to the play and to Paul's portrayal. For the excitement extended beyond Robeson to Margaret Webster's direction, described as a *tour de force,* to young Ferrer's outstanding Iago and to Hagen's sensitive Desdemona. Within two months the revival had surpassed the previous record of fifty-seven performances set in 1926 when Walter Hampden played the Moor in blackface. Before it finally closed, *Othello* would tally a record run of 296 performances and 494,839 admissions.

XII:
Riding High

With *Othello,* Paul's personal success reached a zenith. To blacks, he was a hero, a giant, so celebrated that on June 1, 1943, when Atlanta's Morehouse College became the first black college to award him an honorary doctorate, President Benjamin E. Mays said simply: "Ladies and gentlemen, I have said again and again: A great man needs no introduction. I give you Paul Leroy Robeson!" Then Mays applauded "the leadership of a man who embodies all the hopes and aspirations of the Negro race and who, despite crippling restrictions, breathes the pure air of freedom."

To whites, Paul was more than ever the symbolic black, and they were willing to listen to his views on any number of subjects. The *New York Herald-Tribune* asked him to speak at the first session of its Forum on Current Problems at the Waldorf-Astoria. When he faced the gathering on November 16, it was not only as Paul Robeson the actor and singer, but also as the chairman of the Council on African Affairs.

The work of the Council was so important to Paul that he turned down an offer of $10,000 for concerts in four New England cities because they conflicted with meetings organized by the Council in San Francisco and Los Angeles. That November day in New York, on the Council's behalf, he talked about his visits to the Soviet Union, where he found "new life, not death, freedom, not slavery, true human dignity, not inferiority of status," and he linked the problems of American blacks to the problems of other minorities and other nations. Since the Ethiopian war, he said, the American black had been impressed with "the parallel between his own interests and those of oppressed peoples abroad" as he struggled against the forces barring him from full participation in American life. The three things that caused the most bitter resentment among black Americans were, he said: economic insecurity resulting from continuing discrimination in urban communities; the segregation and inferior status assigned to Negroes in the armed forces, and their complete exclusion from most of the women's auxiliary services; and the southern poll tax system, which maintained undemocratic elements of authority "not only below the Mason-Dixon line but in our national life as a whole."

In the recent election of his friend Ben Davis, Jr., the black communist, to the city council of New York, he saw a general trend among blacks to vote for the candidate, rather than the party label, and the development of a clear understanding of "their goals, their allies and their enemies." They know, Robeson said, "that those sections of organized labor which have enlisted membership on a plane of strict equality constitute the Negro people's chief allies . . . and they know, too, that the winning of the war against fascism is the first and fundamental requirement towards the realization of a democratic America." As an American, he felt it his duty, he said, to press for "collaboration and friendship now and in the postwar world" . . . with Soviet Russia because Negroes "hate fascism to the death," and the Soviet people were "the most potent and self-sacrificing . . ." of all of the "destroyers" of fascism. He concluded with the words of President Roosevelt on the 1941 signing of the Atlantic Charter: "We are determined that we shall gain total victory over our enemies, and we recognize the fact that our enemies are not only Germany, Italy and Japan: they are all the forces of oppression, intolerance, insecurity and injustice which have impeded the forward march of civilization."

In other speeches Paul performed what was, he was convinced, an important service for the American population—educating it in the meaning of Africa. Africans were playing a vital role in the strategy of the war, and when peace came, they would, like India, demand independence, Paul was sure. Initially, Max Yergan did most of the day-to-day work of the Council he had founded, while Paul lent his voice to raise funds, his prestige to bring audiences, and his charisma to reiterate the Council's message.

About 1943 Dr. W. Alphaeus Hunton, formerly a professor of English at Howard University and politically a Marxist, joined the Council and became editor of its monthly publication, *New Africa*. Another new member, also from Howard, was Doxey A. Wilkerson, at that time a Communist party member whose writings appeared regularly in the party's journal, *Political Affairs*. In the last years of the war the Council's growth continued to spurt upward, and by 1944 there were twenty-two members and five officers, three of whom were black—Robeson, Yergan, and Hunton. The two whites were William Jay Schieffelin and Mrs. Edith C. Field, the wife of millionaire Frederick V. Field, who in early 1944 gave the Council money to move to larger facilities at 23 West 26th Street where it soon established one of the best libraries on African materials in New York. Despite this growth, the Council was never mass-oriented; relatively few people knew of its existence. Yet it was the first predominantly black organization that attempted to influence U.S. policy toward Africa.

One such effort was a conference, "Africa—New Perspectives," sponsored by the Council in 1944, that attracted about 110 persons from labor groups, churches, the NAACP, the National Negro Congress, the National Council of Negro Women, representatives from the Belgian Congo, and from the governments of Liberia, France, and the Soviet Union. Before the group Paul criticized the current description of Africa as "the last great frontier of the world for the white man to cross" and the growing idea that Africa was "the jackpot of World War II." Such an attitude, he said, was useful propaganda for the Japanese enemy. Max Yergan lashed out at imperialism and discrimination, but his overall tone was an idealistic call for black and white liberals to work together. Importantly, he maintained that the solution to African problems must be within the framework of the United Nations.[1]

Paul was an "intense kind of person who had to have identification," recalled Stanley Levinson, a radical lawyer who later helped to found Martin Luther King's Southern Christian Leadership Council. "FDR was making changes, but they weren't enough for a radical-thinking black," said Levinson, who while not a close friend later traveled in some of the same circles as Paul. "I do not mean that he had a technical membership [in the Communist party]. A technical membership was nothing . . . the editor of one of New York's papers was a Communist party member for six months, but he wasn't ideologically committed. Paul was ideologically committed . . ."[2]

Scientific socialism and full citizenship for blacks were the focus of Paul's commitment. During many of his concerts he would sing and talk about the Soviet Union, and he rarely missed an opportunity to speak for blacks. When Baseball Commissioner Kenesaw Mountain Landis held a conference on baseball at the Roosevelt Hotel on December 4, 1943, Paul joined a group of black newsmen to discuss discrimination with ball club owners. Unlike his early collegiate days, he told the owners, when he and Fritz Pollard were setting a precedent for black players, now it was common practice for college teams to have blacks on their rosters. Wasn't it time for the major leagues to add Negro players as well?

These were the years when Paul became very close to W. E. B. Du Bois, whom he had known from his earlier days in Harlem, and who had rejoined the NAACP in 1944 after having broken with the organization years earlier over policy.Robeson looked up to Du Bois, admiring his original thinking and brilliant way of probing intellectual problems, and he sang at several of the birthday dinners for Du Bois. No two men could have had more strikingly different personalities. Du Bois was older, aloof and austere. Paul thought nothing of going into a Harlem restaurant and, between bites, holding court with whoever wandered over to talk to him. His friends ranged from the famous gangster Bumpy Johnson to Park Avenue millionaires downtown.

Robeson was a presence on the West Coast as well. Olga Gow (whose husband James and Arnaud d'Usseau conferred with Paul many times while they were writing *Deep Are the Roots* between 1944 and 1946) recalled musical evenings at the home of her father, a violinist with the Los Angeles Symphony. "Robeson was probably there for the quartets, with Stravinsky, who was in Los Angeles at the time, and Albert Einstein, who played violin (badly)."[3]

A black San Francisco journalist, Mason Roberson, recalled "drinking with him and interviewing him" over the years when he was in town. "I also met him at parties. He was a great friend of Louise R. Berman," the wealthy coffee heiress. Paul often stayed with Noel Sullivan (the hotels were segregated), a great angel of opera and symphony who opened his doors to artists like Langston Hughes and Marian Anderson. Roberson described a typical party: "We were playing 'Spin the Bottle' for fun when Paul got up and herded all of the women into the kitchen. He was so big he blocked the door and he talked to them alone."[4]

That Paul was a hero of the Left, and of oppressed people of all nations, creeds, and colors was never more evident than in April 1944, when an estimated 13,000 people turned out to celebrate his forty-sixth birthday at the Seventeenth Regiment Armory in New York City, with proceeds going to the Council on African Affairs. Sponsors included composer W.C. Handy, playwright Lillian Hellman, Duke Ellington, Joe Louis, and playwright-producer Marc Connelly. Among

Albert A. Freeman

Josh White, Paula Lawrence, Paul Robeson, and Uta Hagen in New York in the
mid-1940s

the speakers was Mrs. Mary McLeod Bethune, who said in behalf of
the National Council of Negro Women: "We recognize you as the
tallest tree of our forest in your courageous field of service. We, the
women of America, bring to you our gratitude for the inspiration
which your daily life affords to all mankind."

Vincente Toledano, president of the Confederation of Mexican
workers, surprised even Paul when he turned up unexpectedly and,
speaking in Spanish, said that Paul and President Roosevelt were the
two most beloved North Americans in his country for their democratic ideals. Paul's friend Dr. William Jay Schieffelin declared: "Paul
Robeson belongs to all of us. The multiplicity of his gifts, the depth of
his heart, and the breadth of his mind have made him the friend—the
honored friend—of people in every walk of life."City Councilman
Benjamin J. Davis, described him as "our friend." "I Know a Man," a
song written for the occasion by Louis Lerman and Sam Mor-

gensterne, was sung by a member of the Philadelphia Opera, while the Bakers Union supplied the five-tier, four-foot cake. Paul was deeply moved, and tears streamed down his cheeks as he thanked his audience.

In May the American Academy of Arts and Letters awarded Paul the Medal for Good Diction on the Stage, and in July Paul received *Billboard's* first annual Donaldson Award for an Outstanding Lead Performance. When *Othello* closed in July, Paul and the cast rested two months before going into rehearsal for a cross-country tour that would last more than six months.

It was during the national run of *Othello* that a romantic fling with Uta Hagen, the beautiful young actress, who had first gained prominence in 1938 as Nina in Chekhov's *The Sea Gull*, had embarrassing consequences for Paul. While the cast was in Detroit, Ferrer burst in on her and Paul in a hotel room, drawing headlines around the country.

There had been snickers for a long time over Essie's "tolerance," but clearly Essie was more concerned with the family relationship. Paul, too, seemed to respect that situation. He had had the opportunity—at times intimates said, even the desire—to cut his marital ties, but he had always been checked by his feeling of responsibility to his family and to his people. He could never forget his father's words about his symbolic role, and these were echoed by some of his friends, who told him that part of the burden of his position was living up to what American blacks expected of him, expectations they did not fulfill themselves. Other friends frankly told Essie to give Paul up. Trade unionist George Murphy, a close friend of the Robesons, remembers Essie saying to him during this period: "You have no idea how warm and good it is to have a friend to talk to who respects me and who may not agree with me but who feels warmly to me. That's very important to me," she went on, in the words of a lonely and misunderstood woman who probably had to endure the hostility of some of Paul's friends—particularly the numerous women who loved him. Yet she expressed no bitterness, only pain, resignation, and a deep attachment to Paul.

A great deal of Paul's time was now devoted to supporting militant labor unions and their cause, and it was, in part, because of this that his patriotism was suspect. Several of the CIO unions were dominated by the procommunist left wing, and in 1944 Republican presidential candidate Thomas E. Dewey charged that communists, acting through

Sidney Hillman, chairman of the CIO's Political Action Committee, had seized control of the American labor movement and "now . . . are seizing control of the Government of the United States." Roosevelt, said Dewey, had auctioned control of the Democratic party to the "highest bidder," that is, Hillman and Earl Browder, in order to perpetuate himself in office. Henry Luce in his widely read publications, was equally rabid on the subject that year. And late in 1944 J.B. Matthews, the ex-red who had much to do with the creation of HUAC in 1938, testifying before the Dies committee at a hearing in Washington, described Hillman's committee as "the most active Communist front organization in the United States." Matthews said he based this conclusion on a study of the names of the 141 National Citizens' Political Action Committee members.

Essie came to Paul's defense and branded the communist charges as "absurdly foolish . . .stupid. Every time you open your mouth people yell Communist. I recognize the noise that you hear every time you do anything that is even remotely intelligent. They used to call us 'black', but now they call us 'red.' "5

Paul meanwhile continued to tour in *Othello*. Chicago was the final city, and the production opened at the Erlanger Theater on April 10, 1945. Two days later Franklin Roosevelt died suddenly. It was an especially stunning blow to black Americans. Even Paul, who according to his friend Hope R. Stevens, didn't find the New Deal reforms enough, considered Roosevelt an exemplary politician and his death a great loss. At a meeting of the Independent Citizens' Committee of the Arts, Sciences and Professions, Paul read an ode that Carl Sandburg had written in Roosevelt's memory.

Less than a month later, while Paul was at a party in his honor, word came that the war in Europe was over. According to Marie Seton, who was also at the party, Paul never seemed happier than on this day.

Sunday mornings in Chicago often found Paul speaking in black and white churches and at synagogues. He talked of the forthcoming United Nations Conference on International Organizations that was to be held in San Francisco from April through June. It was to be the principal event in establishing a new order for the postwar world, and Paul and the Council on African Affairs were deeply interested. The new organization would fight imperialism and fascism more vigorously than the old League of Nations, they hoped.

Throughout the war blacks had fought to eliminate discrimination and maltreatment and to give reality to the ideal of the Four Freedoms at home and abroad. Thus, they naturally looked toward San Francisco to see if the nations of the world could establish an organization that would provide relief to oppressed people everywhere. When the delegates from colonial countries spoke, they seemed to voice the yearnings of the underprivileged. But when the charter was completed on June 26, the Council on African Affairs criticized its failure to establish means for the United Nations to insure the effective and rapid economic, social, and political advancement of colonial peoples throughout the world.

In this period after World War II, more blacks than ever before had a modicum of economic security as a result of the opening up of basic industries and unions to them. Black soldiers returning from the front expected the promises of the war to be kept. Victory meant brotherhood had vanquished racism, didn't it? But they met many of the same reactions that black soldiers had met after World War I: Too many whites feared that black soldiers who had been trained to kill would turn their guns on white Americans. In retaliation some of the modest gains that had been made during the war were withdrawn. The Fair Employment Practices Committee, for example, was killed.

Meanwhile, outside America, the shape of the world was changing. In Africa and Asia imperialism was dying, and with it the centuries-old notion of white supremacy, as new nations began to emerge. These independent nonwhite nations stirred the self-respect of many black Americans, and rekindled feelings for an African past that whites had cynically painted as uncivilized, savage, and worthless. The masses of blacks were catching up to where Paul was trying to lead them in his cultural articles of a decade earlier. "World War II has given to the Negro a sense of kinship with other colored—and also oppressed—peoples of the world," Walter White noted. "Where he has not thought through or informed himself on the racial angles of colonial policy and master race theories, he senses that the struggle of the Negro in the United States is part and parcel of the struggle against imperialism and exploitation in India, China, Burma, Africa, the Philippines, Malaya, the West Indies, and South America."[6]

As soon as the war was over, Paul had dashed to Europe with Larry Brown to entertain troops in the occupied areas. Accompanied by violinist Miriam Solovieff, they were the first racially mixed unit to be sent overseas, and they gave twenty-five concerts for the soldiers in France, Germany, and Czechoslovakia. The tour was a success, but

Paul was disturbed by the reactions of Americans he met in Europe, who seemed anxious to revert to prewar politics. During the war America and Russia had been joined against fascism, and nearly anything Russian, from folk songs to Shostakovich's symphonies to caviar and vodka, became enormously popular. In their idealism many Americans did not perceive the realities of Stalinism, or if they did, were swept along in the bigger tide. But once the war was over, Americans did not even seem to give lip service to the notion of a lasting friendship. The Allied world of unity was at an end.

XIII:
Cold Warrior

With the radicalism of the 1930s and the ideological truce that existed during World War II being brought abruptly to an end, Paul felt he was going to have to dedicate himself even more to the struggle that was shaping up. Robeson's friends in the procommunist left wing, especially in the CIO unions, were routed from the ranks of labor, and other ultraliberal labor leaders publicly broke with communists with whom they had been allied on reform and other issues. The American Communist party too had been "reconstituted" in early July, and Earl Browder expelled, as it turned its back on wartime "national unity" and reverted to earlier, more militant tactics. On the "Negro Question" the program returned to a more carefully stated and conceived version of self-determination. On broader issues it moved from cooperation to all-out opposition to Truman. Leadership of the party passed to William Foster, Harry Winston, Benjamin J. Davis, Jr., and others.

Ben Davis was Paul's "dear friend," and Paul was "always pleased to say so, . . . I admired him, when as a young lawyer in Atlanta, he bravely defended a framed-up Negro youth and eventually won the case (Angelo Herndon); I admired him later when, as a City Councilman in New York, he championed the rights of our people; and I admired him when, during his imprisonment, he began a legal fight to break down the Jim Crow system in the Federal penitentiaries. How could I *not* feel friendly to a man like that?"[1]

Around the world the hot war turned cold. The Russians took the position that they must now hastily erect bastions of protection against a hostile West and did so, setting up eastern European satellites, and stripping Manchuria of its industrial resources. The

Western powers, even before the end of the war, had been making plans to restore the policy of containment, in a complete reversal of the spirit of Yalta. A month after Roosevelt's death Winston Churchill called for "Anglo-American armies" to police the world, and in September 1945 the foreign ministers of the "Big Five" met in London in a quarrelsome discussion over the eastern European satellites, Iran, Italy, and Trieste.

Paul's reaction was swift and outspoken. On November 26 he told the Central Conference of American Rabbis in New York that the United States "has taken over the role of Hitler and now stands for counterrevolution all over the world." His shocked listeners were outraged at his words. Certainly his ideas were controversial at the time, though some have argued that thoughtful whites had made similar statements without causing such a flap. (On a smaller scale, the reaction to his speech was not unlike the rebuke to Martin Luther King, Jr., when he spoke out against Vietnam: "Stick to the Negro question and leave foreign policy to the white experts.") But Paul had always been deeply set against the forces to maintain the status quo, and his views always encompassed all of the world's oppressed people. Paul also said the atomic bomb secrets should be given to the U.S.S.R. "because a strong Russia would be a deterrent against another war."

When Martin Dies did not run for reelection in 1944 and three members of his House Un-American Activities Committee were defeated, many intellectuals and others hoped the group would shut down. But in 1945, instead of dissolving the committee, Congress made it permanent. By the end of the year the new chairman, John E. Rankin of Mississippi, had begun conducting hearings and firing off press releases.

Paul could feel the chilling change in the political atmosphere as he traveled around the country in 1945-1946 giving 115 concerts. It is ironic that that tour and the tours in 1946-1947—those in which Paul reached, to Larry Brown's mind, his greatest peak as a singer—were, for Robeson the man, some of the most difficult years of his life. Paul had never had such receptions in America, nor as many concerts. Yet at no time since before the war did he feel so personally frustrated. "Music has never meant to Paul what it means to me," Larry said. "In other circumstances I doubt if Paul would have been a singer. It's irony that at the peak of his career and at the moment when I think he reached his zenith, he was more difficult to work with than during all the years before. He was in a terrible mood. He constantly felt he could not sing another concert."[2]

Lena Horne and Paul Robeson look over plans for the Council on African Affairs rally at Madison Square Garden, June 1946

In 1946, Paul was elected a vice-president of the Civil Rights Congress along with writer Dashiell Hammett and others. According to Wilson Record, "The bulk of the support came from two sources: the Party organizations such as the National Negro Congress, the Southern Negro Congress, the Southern Negro Youth Congress and the United Negro and Allied Veterans of America and the trade unions under Party control."[3] William L. Patterson took over the job of executive director, while noncommunists held important elective positions. Despite the existence of CRC chapters in some large urban areas, the CRC never had a mass base, but it did effectively picket and work for the civil rights of black Americans at various times during its life.

Paul also continued his activities with the Council on African Affairs, which sponsored conferences and rallies to provide assistance to famine victims in South Africa. Marian Anderson sang at a Council rally in Harlem in January 1946. And in June a mass meeting "for African freedom" in Madison Square Garden was attended by 15,000 persons. On this occasion, as on others, Paul decried the United States practice of getting uranium from the Belgian Congo for atomic bombs; and he reiterated his belief that the race was on in Africa between progress and democracy on the one side and imperialism and reaction on the other. On almost every issue Robeson was at variance with official U.S. foreign policy.

Whatever warmth might still have existed between America and the U.S.S.R. was effectively frozen in March 1946 when Harry S. Truman announced his policy to contain communist expansion and offered to give military aid to peoples fighting to prevent communist takeovers. The image of communist spies lurking in the State Department was to be matched only by the suspicion of those in other government departments. Less than two weeks after announcement of the Truman Doctrine came the Loyalty Order, which placed 2.2 million federal employees under the scrutiny of federal and police investigatory agencies. At the time Paul was in Washington as the Council on African Affairs' delegate to a national conference protesting lynching. He asked Truman's assistant, David K. Niles, to set up a meeting between the President and a delegation from the conference. Paul and others were greeted cordially at the White House. "All right-thinking Americans abhor lynching," the President told them. He had promised Walter White of the NAACP that he would name a commission to look into the subject. But Robeson's delegation found that promise inadequate. One member, Mrs. Harper Sibley, the wife of the former head of the U.S. Chamber of Commerce, wondered aloud whether the United States could rightly take the lead in the Nuremberg trials while justice for blacks was lagging and while lynchings were rampant. By one account, Mrs. Sibley's remarks caused the blood to rush to Truman's face. "Domestic problems are domestic problems and foreign problems are foreign problems," he shot back. Paul responded that the temper of blacks was changing, especially among war veterans. "If they can't have protection [locally] they want to know they will have federal protection." Truman was furious; it seemed that Paul was threatening the President of the United States, and Truman told Paul so. Before the President bade the group a frigid farewell, Paul apologized, explaining that in the depth of his feeling, "I'm afraid I was carried away."

As the delegation was leaving the White House a reporter asked

Robeson the question that had been raised sporadically: "Are you a communist?" "No," said Paul. "I label myself as very violently anti-fascist."

"Paul saw that anticommunism was one of the great weapons in the hands of imperialism," Louise Patterson was to say later. "It was another way, just as racism, of 'divide and rule.' That's the 'why' (of Robeson). That was his great vision."

Two weeks later, on October 7, 1946, Paul again was asked that question, this time by Senator Jack Tenney and the California Joint Fact-Finding Committee on Un-American Activities. The Tenney committee, as it was called, had begun its investigation into alleged left-wing activities in Hollywood, and Paul was brought before it. "Are you a communist?" Robeson testified under oath that he was *not* and had never been a member of the Communist party. Citing the guarantees of the First Amendment to the U.S. Constitution, it would be the last time he would answer the question before an investigating committee.

Was Paul Robeson a member of the Communist party? It is a fact that Paul had a love affair with Soviet Russia and that his affection was repaid in full measure. Why else name a mountain and place his likeness at its peak? Efforts to obtain FBI documents that might have shed further light on this subject were blocked by the Robeson family, but interviews with dozens of intimates counter the contention of one paid FBI informant that Paul was a party member with ambitions to be a "Black Stalin." "In (the thirties) all of the intellectuals were either Marxists or sympathetic to the cause," C. L. R. James recalled in 1967. "Paul was the most distinguished and important one on the world scene who associated himself with it, though he was not a member of the party." Paul said of himself: "The truth is: I am not and never have been involved in any international conspiracy or any other kind, and do not know anyone who is." Although he was ideologically committed to Marxism, Paul was not an organization man. He could be unreasonable, he could be brilliant. His associations and sympathies were without a doubt with the procommunist Left, but it is very doubtful that Paul Robeson ever had a card.

In January 1947 an article in the *New York Times* announced that Paul intended to leave the theater and concert stage to "talk up and down the nation against race hatred and prejudice." He was considering it, but he was not yet ready.

By then, the House Un-American Activities Committee was "bagging," as Chief Investigator Robert E. Stripling was prone to say, suspected communists with increasing frequency. "The Committee considers the Communist Party of the United States to be a subversive organization, and the testimony or activities of any individual connected with the Communist Party of the United States is considered to be in the purview of this Committee's authority," Chairman J. P. Parnell Thomas made clear to stunned witnesses.

Almost as a response Paul interspersed his tours with more and more appearances at political and labor affairs, and he spoke out against racism during his concerts. In January 1947 in St. Louis he told his predominantly white audience it made him "sick inside" that they could hear him sing, but no Negro could enter the theater across the street. Then he joined members of the Civil Rights Conference, who were picketing the American Theater, which barred blacks. "Some of us will have to speak up and appeal to the people to respect the common rights of others. It seems that I must raise my voice but not by singing pretty songs," he told reporters.

And in March 1947 in Salt Lake City, before a concert audience of lower-income people, intellectuals, college students, businessmen, and local civic and government leaders, Paul made a dramatic announcement. "You've heard my final formal concert for at least two years, and perhaps for many more," he said. "I'm retiring here and now from concert work. . . ."

He went on to finish the tour, though, as opposition slammed into him like a wrecking ball. His denial under oath that he was a communist was forgotten; the question became the issue. In Peoria, Illinois, the Shrine Mosque denied him use of their hall, and the mayor even ordered extra police to keep him from entering the city. Shortly afterwards, Albany, New York, canceled the permit it had issued him earlier, but the case was taken to court and Paul eventually sang in that city—without political comment—before 1,100 people. Complaints began to come in to his manager, Fred Schang. A man from the West Coast objected to Paul's Soviet songs, often sung as encores. "It appears to us that Mr. Robeson used his concert as a medium for Communist propaganda, and we feel there is no place in our United States for such propaganda, whether on the concert stage or elsewhere." Under such fire the resolve of Paul's Salt Lake City announcement hardened. His decision had been made when he said there, "I shall sing, from now on, for my trade union and college friends; in other words, only at gatherings where I can sing what I please."

XIV: Progressive Politics

In the fall of 1947, HUAC turned its guns on Hollywood, where hearings began on October 20. Friendly witnesses included Ayn Rand, Adolphe Menjou, Robert Taylor, Ronald Reagan, and Gary Cooper. Of nineteen other witnesses scheduled to appear, eight refused: Larry Parks, Robert Rossen, Waldo Salt, Richard Collins, Gordon Kahn, Howard Koch, Lewis Milestone, Irving Pichel. (Parks, Rossen, and Collins later became friendly witnesses.) Ten, the "Hollywood Ten," appeared and took the Fifth Amendment, refusing to testify: Alvah Bessie, Herbert Biberman, Lester Cole, Edward Dmytryk, Ring Lardner, Jr., John Howard Lawson, Albert Maltz, Samuel Ornitz, Adrian Scott, and Dalton Trumbo. Dmytryk was to become a friendly witness, while Larner and Trumbo later publicly declared themselves ex-communists. The nineteenth, Bertolt Brecht, denied the accusation and immediately left the country.

Lawson's appearance on October 27 provides a telling example of the tenor of the meetings. Lawson asked Representative Thomas if he could read a statement. After looking at it Thomas responded, "I refuse to let you make the statement because of the first sentence." That sentence read: "For a week, this Committee has conducted an illegal and indecent trial of American citizens, whom the Committee has selected to be publicly pilloried and smeared."

Fear was sweeping the country. The few liberals and Democrats who hoped to salvage something of the New Deal froze in their tracks. The movie industry and the publishing industry cringed in fear, as did schoolteachers, artists, writers, scientists, liberals, radicals. Some

Wide World Photos

Robeson speaking at a dinner in honor of Henry A. Wallace (center) given by
the presidential candidate's supporters. Representative Vito Marcantonio of
New York is at left.

people, however, refused to run and hide. Paul was among them.

In December the Attorney General's first list of subversive
organizations was published. It was sweeping, controversial—and,
later historians point out, unconstitutional—and it included the
Council of African Affairs. Nearly thirty years later Howard
University history professor Clarence Contee would chide the notion
that this band of "elite interracial leftists were engaged in any plot to
overthrow the U.S. government," but in the frenzy of the times the
appearance on the "Red List," which was used to deny employment
and impugn loyalty, upset some CAA members and panicked others.

During a tense formal meeting in early 1948—attended by Paul, as
chairman; Max Yergan, the executive director; Mary McLeod
Bethune; William Jay Schieffelin, a founder of the Urban League;
Harlem lawyer Hope R. Stevens; and W. E. B. Du Bois—the red label
was uppermost in everyone's mind. There was nothing new in the

Council's being called "subversive." As early as 1946 the *New York Times*, reporting on Council resolutions condemning imperialism, had said that the "Communists controlled the session." Thus most of these people had grown accustomed to having their militance branded as communism. But at this meeting it soon became clear that Max Yergan wanted to align the Council with American foreign policy to erase its "subversive" label.

Paul was stunned by Yergan's maneuver, and he said he would not retreat one inch from the principles for which he and the Council had worked. Hope Stevens remembers that there always were those among the Council "who felt that Max had headed and developed this organization with something less than enthusiasm for the black man's participation in the struggle for African freedom." After Paul's remarks, Stevens recalls, the board divided along ideological lines, with "Yergan pressing for a softening of stance (on foreign policy) while Robeson was pressing for the outspoken confrontations he felt were necessary for an organization like the Council on African Affairs . . . . Paul regarded the freedom of Africa as affecting the Freedom of Africans in America 100 percent. He didn't care what the label was, and in those days the most vibrant direction to the black man's struggle in America came from men who were communist-trained. He did not shy away from anybody because of his communist affiliation as long as the individual was concerned with and ready to fight for the freedom of black people and of working people." Yergan was outvoted at that meeting and again at a meeting the following month when he tried a similar tactic.

Despite his dramatic announcement at Salt Lake City a year before, Paul did another concert tour in 1948. This one, which took him to Jamaica, turned out to be the last one managed by Columbia, and this time Fred Schang had to assure the Caribbean sponsors that Paul would sing, not politicize. Despite continued complaints and mounting opposition to his appearances, audiences still came; Paul was even given a hero's welcome at Montego Bay.

In late January 1948 he went to the McAlpin Hotel in New York for a meeting that would turn out to have great significance in his life. Gathered there on this blustery day were the many well-known people who, for a variety of reasons, wanted an alternative to both the Democratic and Republican parties in the upcoming presidential campaign. Out of this group emerged the Henry Wallace for President Committee, which included Paul Robeson; Elmer A. Benson, former Farmer-Labor governor of Minnesota; Braintruster Rexford G. Tugwell, University of Chicago professor and governor of Puerto Rico under FDR; Angus Cameron, editor-in-chief of Little, Brown and Company; and sculptor Jo Davidson.

Former Vice President Wallace had been the last New Dealer to leave the Truman Cabinet. Labeled the "visionary" dreamer of the New Deal who wanted to bestow "a quart of milk on every Hottentot," as Secretary of Agriculture, he later was Truman's Secretary of Commerce and the choice target of conservatives. With the Cold War Wallace had grown increasingly critical of administration policy and seemed a natural choice to head a third party. The rest of the ticket took shape when Senator Glen Taylor of Idaho announced his decision to run for Vice President with Wallace. He was happy to have the support "of all those who go along with our program," Taylor said, but warned the communists that the Progressive purpose was to make the economy work so well that communism would repel Americans. "Henry Wallace is the only leader capable of ending the Cold War and reestablishing even the beginnings of international goodwill (who) had not sought the cheap applause of the reactionary press by blaming all our troubles on Russia," Taylor said.

Paul's appearance on the Wallace committee had an electrifying effect on some blacks, particularly young idealists. No black had ever been given a key role in developing a national political party program, with the exception of the Communist party. Indeed, there were only two blacks in Congress in 1948. "There was a great deal of black support for Henry Wallace," recalls Carl Rowan, who was a fledgling reporter at the time. "I would have loved for the Progressives to win myself. Coleman Young (now mayor of Detroit) was a big supporter of Wallace."

When delegates from across the country met in Chicago's Knickerbocker Hotel in April to officially organize an alternative party, Paul introduced Henry A. Wallace as the leader of the Progressives and voiced his hope that he would be nominated as the party's candidate to oppose Truman and Thomas E. Dewey in November. Wallace's nomination, of course, was a foregone conclusion. The more difficult issues at the Progressive party convention— held in Philadelphia in July—were debated at the committee meetings and concerned the committee reports for the platform. From the start the convention split over the issue of communism.

The subcommittee to draft the preliminary platform, for example, included Martin Popper, executive secretary of the National Lawyers Guild, as chairman; Essie Robeson; Louis Adamic; Joseph E. Johnson, a dean of Howard University; and Professor Frederick L. Schuman of Williams College. Immediately, Cedric Thomas, a real estate man from Maine also on the committee, moved to include in the platform Glen Taylor's statement repudiating communism. Essie Robeson and Popper objected, declaring that that would amount to redbaiting; eventually, the motion was defeated.

The battle continued on other questions, however. The committee also had to consider whether Soviet foreign policy should be criticized, since a plank had been adopted in which U.S. policy was roundly condemned. Schuman prepared an amendment that read, "We demand that the United States stop sacrificing the cause of peace to industrial profits and military ambition. We demand that the Soviet Union stop sacrificing the cause of peace to territorial aggrandizement and power politics." Reportedly, someone told Schuman that if this statement were offered, "Paul Robeson would object from the floor and declare the second sentence untrue." Schuman modified the proposal to say that the threat to world peace was the "joint responsibility of the Soviet Union and the United States," and this was the version Wallace, and the convention, finally approved.

When the work of the convention moved out onto the floor, Robeson's own charisma become evident. In her biography Marie Seton said the cry of "Robeson for Vice-President" was picked up in the hall. It is difficult to tell whether this "spontaneous outburst" was a stage-managed element or not. Certainly, there was no serious move to elect Paul, and he himself had no intention of running for political office. That his presence had an electrifying effect, however, is evident in the recollection of a young soldier who attended the convention during a leave in Philadelphia: "I was politically naive and didn't know anything of what was happening, but I was absolutely enthralled at the sight of a giant black man on the stage, having an input. I have never forgotten that thrill."[1]

Throughout these months before the nomination and up to the election Paul continued his political activities in other areas as well, but most of his efforts were meeting with frustration. In February 3,000 persons attending a meeting in his honor at the Friendship Baptist Church sent a telegram to President Truman asking him to order Attorney General Clark to cease deportation proceedings against Alex

Balint, regional director of the Mine, Mill and Smelter Workers Union, CIO, ostensibly for visa irregularities but actually for his politics, and grant him immediate citizenship status.

In mid-May Paul joined W. E. B. Du Bois, Roscoe Dungee of the Oklahoma *Black Dispatch*, and others in requesting an appointment with President Truman in June for representatives of a "National non-partisan delegation of several hundred citizens from labor, civic, religious and other organizations" to confer with the chief executive "regarding urgency of immediate passage of anti-poll tax, anti-lynching and fair employment legislation." The President's secretary, Matthew J. Connally, replied that the group could not see the President.

On September 21, Paul himself wired President Truman requesting an appointment for a "delegation of Negro leaders to present a 'Statement of Negro Americans' signed by nearly 600 citizens throughout the country." A member of the White House staff replied tersely: "Unable to Make Appointment You Requested."

The refusal was not unexpected. When the Senate had opened hearings on the Mundt-Nixon Bill, which required all Communist party members to register, declared them ineligible for federal employment, denied them passports, and subjected them to immediate deportation if they were aliens, Paul had gone to Washington on June 1 to testify against the bill. Chairman Homer Ferguson asked Paul several times if he was a communist. Each time Paul replied that he would "answer that" question in due course. Finally, Paul said, "The question has become the very basis of the struggle for civil liberties. Nineteen men are about to go to jail for refusing to answer it. I am prepared to join them. I refuse to answer it."[2]

Robeson called "too hypothetical" a query about his willingness to fight against Russia if Congress declared war. As to whether he would fight Russia, that "would depend on many things."

"Then you would be the judge?" another committeeman asked.

"No, no, a lot of people would be the judges," Paul replied.

For the Wallace campaign, Paul stumped up and down the country, speaking at rallies and by some accounts, growing increasingly strident. *The New York Times* said Robeson cried out at a Washington rally, "We have taken the offensive against fascism! We will take the power from their hands and through our representatives we will direct the future destiny of our nation." Campaigning took him into the deep South—an extremely dangerous place for a black man with so radical a domestic and foreign policy. (Wallace himself— speaking out against racial discrimination—was traveling through a hail of rotten tomatoes and eggs.) Six-foot-three-inch Paul Robeson was a sure target for the Ku Klux Klan. Before one meeting at a church in Memphis, Tennessee, the Klan mobilized in the hills. Only a few local blacks showed up, but the Memphis black community insisted that Wallace and Robeson be given a detachment of black police as guards. When night fell, the Klan, dressed in their white robes and caps, drove up in their cars, but to their shock, they found over a hundred black men from the fields standing "silent and ready." The Klansmen did not stop.

By early summer Essie too was on a whirlwind three-week tour, stumping with Wallace in fifteen states. She entitled her windup speech in New Haven, in her home state of Connecticut, "Double Talk." In it she declared she was not a communist but had her own ideas and convictions about American law and freedom and loyalty, having grown up in an America that did not practice what it so eloquently preached. She detailed the persistent persecution of her people. "Some people are disconcerted, frightened and confused by it, but not I." She reiterated her American citizenry and her intention to remain in the country.

She, Paul, and W. E. B. Du Bois were coming to be the only notable blacks still supporting Wallace in what was, of course, a futile try for the Presidency. As the Progressives got an increasingly bad press— with charges of "communist-inspired" and "communist-dominated" gaining credibility—black leaders such as Walter White and A. Philip Randolph, who had at first endorsed the third party, started speaking out against Wallace. Their opinion—or at least their decision not to support the Progressives—was echoed at the polls in November, when more blacks voted for Truman, the winning candidate, than for Wallace.

It was a defeat for Paul, too, coming at a time when he seemed to meet obstacles at every turn. The Transport Workers Union in New York— whose leader had been known as "Red Mike" Quill in the days when being a radical was not equated with being a traitor—refused to let Robeson speak. And in a terrible foreshadowing of what was to come, a West Virginia library banned a children's biography, *Paul Robeson: Citizen of the World*, from its shelves.

XV:
Paris Aftermath

In February 1949, finding engagements hard to obtain in the United States, Paul left for a concert tour in England. He wanted "to make it perfectly clear that the world is wide, and a few pressures (will) not stop my career." It was a triumphant return for him after a decade. In Manchester, two hours after tickets for his concert were put on sale, all 10,000 seats were sold. He put his time in England to political use too. He sang and spoke for South African and other causes, and in April he attended a meeting of the Coordinating Committee of Colonial Peoples in London, together with Dr. Y.M. Dadoo, president of the South African Indian Congress. That group of 2,000 students from various parts of the colonial world, from populations that ranged from 6 to 700 million people, asked him to speak in its name when he went to the Partisans of Peace's World Peace Congress in Paris, a request destined to have stunning reverberations.

There, in an unwritten speech, Paul told the congress that the colonial peoples denounced the policy of the U.S. government, "which is similar to that of Hitler and Goebbels," and in their search for peace and liberty would fight for them along with the Soviet Union, the democracies of Eastern Europe, China and Indonesia. Then he went on to say, "It is unthinkable . . . that American Negroes would go to war on behalf of those who have oppressed us for generations . . . against a country (the Soviet Union) which in one generation has raised our people to full human dignity of mankind."

His remarks made headlines all over America. He was widely attacked, and his remarks, taken out of context, misinterpreted as "treason." The *Washington Post* wrote, "If he had said that his first loyalty was to his own country, it would have been difficult to believe him. When he said, however, that his views are shared by Negroes generally, he was actually betraying them in the interest of Communist tactics to the advocates of white supremacy." "Ungrateful and disloyal," the *New York Journal-American* called him. The Council on African Affairs sent a telegram to him in Paris detailing the flap he had caused, "but Paul couldn't understand what was going on . . . what everybody was getting so stirred up about," recalled Louise Patterson, who by then had joined the Council staff. A dozen years later, Paul wrote in his book, *Here I Stand:*

> As I spoke, I thought of the 40,000,000 blacks in South America and the West Indies; of the 15,000,000 of my people in America, and of the 150,000,000 in Africa. We delegates had resolved that we would be willing to fight for peace, but that we were not interested in perpetuating and extending the powers of the dominant one per cent which controls our civilization . . . I definitely did not say I was speaking for 15,000,000 colored Americans, but as the controversy turned out to be so internationally significant, I am certainly asking no corrections.

Many letters and telegrams arrived at the White House, protesting Paul's statements, as reported in the press, and declaring that blacks would, indeed, fight against Russia. The Interdenominational Minister's Alliance of Greater Little Rock, Arkansas, wrote that "The reported statement of Paul Robeson does not meet the approval of intelligent American Negroes." A Joplin, Missouri, businessman wrote that Paul should be given a one-way ticket to the Soviet Union. "Black Russian skunk," said one letter. "Why can't our government find some way to take this Russian-dominated over-educated, black fool into 'protective custody'? . . . He is . . . the first black Benedict Arnold in our country," it continued. And a St. Louis letter to Attorney General Tom Clark drawled: "How about a treason charge or something similar against this Nigger Robeson?" A Philadelphia man was more to the point, however, when he wondered if, in the army's continued adherence to segregation, it was trying "to persuade Negroes to support Paul Robeson or Jackie Robinson?"[1]

Paul continued his European tour, despite the denouncements that rained on him from America, but he was an increasingly angry man. His words and actions were being taken out of proper context by the media in America, he felt. For example, when he arrived at his next stop, Stockholm, on April 21 many reporters were among the welcoming group, but the American correspondents' cables to their papers stressed that two writers from the Swedish communist newspapers were there. Paul told an Oslo news conference that he fully expected that his political opinions and speeches might one day land him in jail. Yet he didn't budge on his convictions. In Copenhagen later in April, he canceled concerts when he learned that the sponsoring newspaper, *Politiken*, supported the Atlantic Treaty. He would not sing until another sponsor was found.

From Copenhagen Paul went back to Britain, where he launched a series of low-priced "workman's concerts" at Gateshead, Liverpool, Manchester, Sheffield, and in Clydebank.[2] The strain of the concerts and the tension was telling on Larry Brown. For the first time in his twenty-four-year association with Paul, he begged off finishing the rest of the tour. Pleading complete exhaustion, he returned to America. Thus, for the remainder of the trip Paul's accompanist was a white South African named Bruno Raikin.

Near the end of May Robeson went on to Czechoslovakia for four days of concerts. After one evening performance at the stadium, he talked in Prague with young Chinese, Indonesian, and Canadian blacks until 3:00 A.M. It was then he told Marie Seton, who had arrived three days after him, that he expected a difficult fight ahead of him in America. "I don't know if I'll live to see the end of the struggle. I've overcome my fear of death. I never think about death now."[3] Finally, in June, Paul concluded his tour with concerts in Russia, in time for the 150th anniversary of Pushkin's birth.

When Robeson returned to New York on June 16, he was met by about sixty supporters, a battery of reporters, and at least six uniformed policemen. Faced with their questions, he promised to clarify his Paris statements at a rally to be staged by the Council on African Affairs on June 19, at the Rockland Palace in Harlem. He also agreed to a press conference and reportedly snapped at reporters who objected to his followers' attending it, so annoyed was he by now with what he felt were distortions of his statements by the press. When asked about a news story from Moscow that quoted him as saying he "loved the Soviet Union," Paul interrupted with, "Who said that?" Did he deny it? "Don't give me any leading questions," he reportedly retorted. "What I said was that I love the America of which I am a part. I don't love the America of your press." He felt a small "clique of financial despots" was trying to plunge the country into war. After the press conference a twenty-five-car motorcade took Paul across the Triborough Bridge and through the streets of Harlem, where signs on the cars announced the "Welcome Home Rally" on Sunday.

Sunday also marked the wedding day for Paul, Jr., now nearly twenty-two, and Marilyn Greenberg, whom he had met two years before at Cornell University, where he had been a football hero. The interracial marriage would be a special burden for any couple, but Paul, Jr., was sure that Marilyn's Jewish background gave the two of them a special understanding.[4] The two had decided on a quiet wedding in the home of a minister, with Paul and Essie and Marilyn's mother and brother, but the interracial ceremony and Paul's current notoriety made his son's wedding news. Arriving at the minister's apartment building, Paul, Sr., found reporters and photographers gathered outside and became furious. "I have the greatest contempt for the democratic press," he hissed as he made his way through the crowd, "only something within me keeps me from smashing your cameras over your heads. It is my intention to block off the couple to prevent you from making pictures of them."

By the time the vows were spoken, several hundred people had joined the journalists. They watched as the couple and their families came out of the apartment, some of them hissing and booing Pauli and Marilyn. Robeson sputtered with rage when reporters poked their cameras into the cab that was taking the couple away.

Later that evening at the Rockland Palace rally Robeson was greeted by a crowd estimated from about 3,500 to 5,000. In a ninety-minute speech he was quoted as saying, among other things, that he loved "the Soviet people more than any other nation because of their sufferings and sacrifices for us, the Negro people, the progressive people, the people of the future of the world."

In July 1949 the House Un-American Activities Committee conducted hearings on communist infiltration of minority groups.[5] Paul, because of his outspoken stands and his visibility, was an easy target. A black undercover investigator for the committee, Alvin W. Stokes, testified that hardly more than 1,400 Negroes, one tenth of 1 percent of the entire Negro population of the United States, were members of the Communist party. He had attended the welcome home rally for Paul, he said, and pointed out that the audience there was over 75 percent white. Turning to attack Robeson himself, he introduced exhibits from the committee's own records, files, and publications, going back to 1936, when *Soviet Russia Today* printed Paul's friendly sentiments to the Soviet Union. There were also news articles and pamphlets in which Paul talked about Russia, as well as documents linking him with organizations later declared by the Attorney General to be "subversive."

Rabbi Benjamin Schultz, national executive director of the American Jewish League vs. Communism, also told the committee that Paul's "attempted provocation of American Negroes" against America and toward Russia was part of a communist conspiracy to inflame racial and religious minorities and eventually set them against one another.

Schultz was only one in a parade of witnesses who denounced Paul's alleged statements in Paris: Thomas W. Young, president and general manager of the Guide Publishing Co., when asked if Paul should be subpoenaed, said that Robeson would only use the hearing "as a sounding board for his own ideas." Lester Granger of the Urban League testified that he didn't bother to attend the Robeson homecoming rally because, "I knew in advance what was going to be said, and I saved the time." Dr. Charles S. Johnson, president of Fisk University, also discounted Robeson's statements.

Jackie Robinson took off his Brooklyn Dodgers uniform, traveled to Washington, and told HUAC, "I can't speak for 15 million people any more than any other one person can; but I know that I've got too much invested for my wife and child and myself in the future of this country, and I and many other Americans have too much invested in our country's welfare, for any of us to throw it away for a siren song in bass."

Not all blacks responded negatively. The *Afro-American* noted in an editorial that Jackie Robinson had been invited "to call Paul Robeson a 'liar' and stated his willingness to fight. So will millions of other colored boys. But there will be some who will not fight for Uncle Sam." Noting that some other blacks thought the Ku Kluxers and bigots more dangerous than the Russians, the editorial said Paul was as good an American as Jackie, who "cannot begin to fill Paul Robeson's shoes." Robinson thinks of himself, it continued; Paul thinks of "millions of colored people in the South who can't vote, who are terrorized by mobs at the least provocation . . . and cannot get a decent job or a decent education."

The most damning testimony before the committee was given July 14, 1949, by Manning Johnson, a black man, who testified under oath that he was a former high-ranking member of the Communist party, educated and trained by communists, but who later left in disgust over their racial and other policies. Johnson said that Paul was a member of the party and had been for many years. "In the Negro commission of the national committee of the Communist Party we were told, under threat of expulsion, never to reveal that Paul Robeson was a member of the Communist Party because Paul Robeson's assignment was highly confidential and secret." He went on to say that Paul wanted to be "the black Stalin among Negroes."

Eight years later Paul commented on Manning Johnson's testimony.

> *The only evidence ever given that I was a communist was given by Manning Johnson, who said I was a party member in 1934 or 1935. I was in England at the time, so he couldn't have been in any cell with me. He has turned out to be such a liar that even the witch-hunters had to disavow him.*
>
> *Now the Communist Party was a legal party, and if I'd wanted to join a political party I might well have picked the Communist Party. I'd never had anything to do with the Democrats or Republicans. But I was not a member of the Communist Party.*[6]

In the wake of the hearings in Washington, the enigmatic Max Yergan also denounced Paul's Paris statement. He said the American Communist party had not raised blacks—or even black communists, whom he called miserable cowards—to the "full dignity of mankind." It had never even touched the majority of the black population, he insisted. Yergan had Mrs. Mary McLeod Bethune tell President Truman's administrative assistant, David K. Niles, that he wished to see him, and Paul was presumably on their agenda when the two met at the White House in late May 1950.

Paul was disgusted by the black leaders who spoke against him. He felt that they failed to understand what he was trying to accomplish for black people, that the Negro leadership was letting him down by blasting him without even talking to him. They hadn't even bothered to find out what he had really said, he argued, and why he had said it. Yes, he was part of the left, part of the progressive world, and had come to political consciousness through the Marxist vision. An internationalist, his world view put him out of step with the more parochial views of traditional black leaders. But there was no effective Third World in those days, no socialist country other than the Soviet Union. Liberation of blacks in Africa and America was for Robeson a possibility only because of the Soviet example where, he believed, an oppressed class had been able to change a whole system and to benefit from it.

For their part Negro leaders felt he had let them down, adding the burden of being "red" to that of being black. Why, they asked, did he insist on attaching what seemed to be naive praise of Russia to every criticism of the United States that was valid independent of references to the Soviet Union?

"When you think of it, even in all of its distorted versions that made the papers and became the thing that precipitated the whole move or fight of terror against Paul," commented Louise Patterson in 1974, staring out of the window of her Harlem apartment, "you'd say, 'What made people even think about it, in light of what some of these nationalists are out here saying today?'"

XVI: An Artist Besieged

Peekskill, in the northwest corner of Westchester County about thirty-five miles from Manhattan, was a typical middle-sized New York State town in 1949. In contrast to the manicured, well-to-do commuters' villages of southern Westchester, Peekskill still retained its rural character. Residents had fought to keep industry out, and job opportunities were scarce, which meant that the town and its surrounding area were cut off from the general prosperity of such nearby cities as Yonkers and politically and economically outside the mainstream of urban American life. As farming became increasingly unprofitable, and the young left for the cities, owners of large tracts of land sold them for resort development, and for years there had been an annual invasion of summer "colonists" from New York. In 1949 there were at least 25,000 vacationers—mostly Jewish merchants, lawyers, doctors, and professionals in the arts—and the 18,000 local residents, whose town served as a shopping center, had become increasingly dependent on them for income.

The summer visitors were not terribly unlike most Peekskill residents, but the majority of native families considered the New York Jews different in customs and thought patterns. The painters, dancers, musicians, and writers lived simply and cheaply, a few even in shacks. Politically, too, the summer residents were different. In the fall of 1948, 4,004 citizens of Peekskill voted for Dewey, 2,555 for President Truman, and none for Henry Wallace.

In contrast, thirty years before, a group of Philosophic Anarchists

had founded a colony in nearby Mohegan. Later, following the
Russian Revolution and the organization of a Communist party in the
United States, a communist summer colony was established near
Beacon, about ten miles from Peekskill, and in the mid-1930s, a
socialist summer colony was established in the Shrub Oak section.

The colonists made almost no attempt to influence the politics of
Peekskill and vicinity, but the differences were aggravated by varying
cultural customs—the summer people concentrating on arts,
literature, and music as opposed to the block dances and competitive
parades that held the attention of most Peekskill residents.

The influx of summer residents also caused traffic jams, crowded
stores, and some disruption of the quiet town's life, prompting anti-
Semitic remarks among the local people. By 1949 the overcrowded
stores had led the summer residents to open shops in the tiny summer
townships, causing Peekskill merchants even to lose their economic
advantage from the "colonists."

On Tuesday, August 23, 1949, in the dry underbrush of growing
hostility to the summer residents, nationwide anti-communist
hysteria, and Paul Robeson's increasing notoriety, the town's only
newspaper, the Peekskill *Evening Star*, ran a front-page news story that
reported:

> Paul Robeson, noted Negro singer and in recent months an avowed
> disciple of Soviet Russia, will make his third appearance in three
> years. . . . Sponsoring the concern is "Peoples Artists, Inc.," an
> organization listed as subversive and branded a Communist front by
> the California Committee on Un-American Activities in 1948.
> Funds collected by sale of tickets will be used for the benefit of the
> Harlem chapter of Civil Rights Congress which has been cited as
> subversive by former U.S. Attorney General Tom Clark.

In the same issue ran an editorial that said:

> It appears that Peekskill is to be "treated" to another concert visit by
> Paul Robeson, renowned Negro baritone. Time was when the honor
> would have been ours—all ours. As things stand today, like most
> folks who put America first, we're a little doubtful of the "honor,"
> finding the luster in the once illustrious name of Paul Robeson now
> almost hidden by political tarnish. . . .
>
> The local concert will be held this coming Saturday at the
> Lakeland Acres Picnic Grounds. The singer is being presented by the
> People's Artists for the benefit of the Harlem Chapter Civil Rights
> Congress according to posters appearing in the neighborhood . . .

Robeson, surrounded by supporters, at the second Peekskill concert, September 4, 1949

*It becomes evident that every ticket purchased for the Peekskill concert
will drop nickels and dimes into the till basket of an Un-American
political organization.*

   *If the Robeson "concert" this Saturday follows the pattern of its
predecessors, it will consist of an unsavory mixture of song and
political talk by one who has described Russia as his "second
motherland" and who has avowed "the greatest contempt for the
democratic press."*

   *The time for tolerant silence that signifies approval is running
out. Peekskill wants no rallies that support iron curtains,
concentration camps, blockades and NKVD's, no matter how
masterful the decor, nor how sweet the music.*

Finally, there was a letter, dated August 18, and written by Vincent J.
Boyle, commander of the Verplanck Post of the American Legion. It
read: "They are coming here to induce others to join their ranks and it
is unfortunate that some of the weaker minded are susceptible to their
fallacious teachings unless something is done by the loyal Americans
of this area." Boyle recalled that the Ku Klux Klan had been run out of
town a few years earlier. "I am not intimating violence in this case, but
I believe that we should give this matter serious consideration and
strive to find a remedy . . . with the same result that they will never
reappear in this area." The concert was scheduled to be held at the
Lakeland Acres Picnic Ground, Boyle pointed out, across the road
from the cemetery where many soldiers were buried. "Are we, as loyal
Americans, going to forget these men and the principles they died for
or are we going to follow their beliefs and rid ourselves of the
subversive organization?"

   The issue of the newspaper sold out.

   By the next day several local groups had picked up the attack. The
President of the Peekskill Chamber of Commerce issued a statement
attacking the concert, and the Junior Chamber of Commerce, labeling
it "un-American," called for "group action" to "discourage it." Alan M.
Grant, supervisor of the town of Cortlandt, in which the concert was
actually to be held, said he was "openly opposed to such gatherings."
Leonard Rubenfeld, assistant county district attorney and chairman of
the Joint Veterans' Council, announced that he had called a meeting of
his group, which included members of the American Legion, Veterans
of Foreign Wars, Catholic War Veterans, and Jewish War Veterans,
and would discuss the Robeson concert. The Verplanck Post of the
American Legion announced it was going to picket the concert and was
asking veterans from neighboring town posts to "cooperate."

On August 26 the Joint Veterans' Council urged its members to join in a parade and a peaceful demonstration. "We can thus illustrate the democratic form of expression and protest in contrast to the force and violence as practiced in communistic and dictatorship countries," the group declared.

By then the concert was being made the occasion for a "holy crusade against communism," and the threat of violence had grown so widespread that the *Peekskill Evening Star*, which had helped fan the flames, was worried. "We strongly commend the local veterans' groups on their plan for PEACEFUL PROTEST. Violence? Absolutely not! Let such tactics remain elsewhere—in the trick bags of the undemocratic," said a two-column editorial on its front page.

Meanwhile, some summer residents, sensing the heightening atmosphere of violence, telegraphed the attorney general of New York State, Westchester County Executive Herbert Gerlach, and County District Attorney George Fanelli urging investigation of the "inflammatory" statements and their authors and protection of the concert, its artist, its sponsors, and its guests. Gerlach telegraphed back that he had referred the matter to the district attorney's office, who said he was referring the matter to local authorities.

On Saturday evening, August 27,[1] a few people arrived at the picnic grounds as early as six o'clock, though the concert was not scheduled to begin until eight. Shortly after seven, nearly fifty carloads of demonstrators had arrived, led by John Zimmer, commander of the Peekskill Post of the Veterans of Foreign Wars, and Robert J. Field, the Westchester county clerk. With an American Legion truck and a stone barricade, the legionnaires blocked the entrance, trapping within the picnic grounds everyone who had arrived early.

Outside, on the highway, the veterans groups paraded, horns blared, bands played, and for two miles back into Peekskill the cars of demonstrators, spectators, and concert-goers were jammed fender to fender. Inside the grounds, when a group of twenty-five Robeson supporters pushed slowly down one road that led from the grounds, they encountered 200 to 300 protesters. Fist-swinging broke out, knocking some of the Robeson supporters to the ground. Several hundred yards further down the road concert-goers stopped, and with their backs to a truck parked across the road, they joined arms and faced the anti-Robeson protestors who tore down a wooden railing and tossed the planks into the group.

At this point "three sheriffs appeared," said leftist writer Howard

Fast, who was on the concert grounds. They argued "half-heartedly" with the protestors, he said, but did not disperse them. A second attack came at 7:30, when about 300 demonstrators, wielding knives, fenceposts, and billy clubs pressed toward the Robeson supporters. Four people were injured, and the concert-goers were driven back, but held fast.

At 7:45 a dozen protesters attacked the women and children among the Robeson supporters who were gathered on the bandstand. The Robeson supporters drove a truck into a strategic position to barricade the road. By now the protesters numbered over 500, and between 7:45 and 8:15 they attacked the Robeson supporters twice but could not break their ranks. "They had worked themselves into a screaming alcoholic frenzy," said Fast, "and they repeated their threats that no one would leave the picnic grounds alive . . . they tore up the fence rails and used them as weapons."

Shortly after eight, protesters burned a twelve-foot cross on the picnic grounds. On at least three separate occasions concert-goers defending the road and bandstand made their way out of the ambush to telephone the local police, the state police, the state attorney general's office, and Governor Dewey—all to no avail.[2] At 8:15 an eyewitness, a man identified later only as H.K., went to telephone the state police. Out on the highway he saw a long line of cars waiting in the dark and one black man and two whites approaching the entrance to the picnic grounds. A mob of protesters stopped them and began pushing them around. Then about a dozen men detached themselves from the mob and pushed the black up against an embankment. H.K. followed. The black man kept saying, "I'm an American! I have a right to attend this concert!" Suddenly, one of the men struck him, and as the black went down, the gang piled on top of him, beating him unmercifully, kicking him in the body, and stepping on his neck. Hoping to stop the violence, H.K. said to a bystander in a soldier's uniform, "Come on buddy, this ain't right." The soldier replied, "That's right, this ain't the American way," and helped to break up the fight, allowing H.K. to half drag the black man through some parked cars and into the woods. "If I hadn't," he said later, "I think they would have murdered him."

By now it was a little after nine. Back on the picnic grounds forty people formed a tight half-circle against the bandstand, with women and children inside and men and boys outside. There they stood and sang, "The Star Spangled Banner," "God Bless America," and "Solidarity Forever."

A few yards away the mob made a bonfire of their books, music, and pamphlets, "circling the fire, screaming obscenities, smashing chairs, and tossing them onto the fire," witness Fast wrote. Not until ten o'clock did the police arrive to bring order.

Robeson had traveled alone to Peekskill by train earlier in the day and had been met at the station, but he was unable to enter the picnic grounds. "About ten o'clock people started to come back to the house and talk about the violence," said Louise Patterson, whose family was among the summer residents.

In the following few days, the leaders of the veterans groups and town officials commented on the affair, some trying to play it down, others boasting. "Our objective was to prevent the Paul Robeson concert," Milton Flynt, commander of the Peekskill Post 274 American Legion, told the *Ossining Citizen Register*, "and I think our objective was reached." Others wrote disagreeing letters to the editor, calling upon the Attorney General to investigate the violence.

District Attorney Fanelli, requested by Governor Dewey to submit a full report on the riot in Peekskill, commented that he didn't know anything about the disorders but was sure the concert-goers, and not the veterans or hoodlums who attacked them, were responsible.

Robeson supporters responded vigorously; 1,500 residents of Westchester County assembled on the grounds of an estate in Katonah, owned by Sam and Helen Rosen, who were among Paul's closest friends. (Sam Rosen had first met Paul when Paul was at Rutgers and Sam was at Syracuse.) There they formed the Westchester Committee for Law and Order. Representatives from thirty communities gathered and invited Robeson to sing in Peekskill again. "We refuse to abandon any section of the United States to organized hoodlums. Our freedom and civil rights are at stake."[3]

The committee announced that a second Robeson concert would be held on Sunday, September 4, at 2:00 P.M. on the grounds of the Hollow Brook Country Club, half a mile from the scene of the previous violence. Their announcement interrupted a meeting of the Verplanck Veterans, who were framing a resolution asking for retraction of the right of assemblage for communist-line organizations. They replied by planning a mammoth protest parade of over 30,000 veterans outside the second concert.

The *Peekskill Star* and District Attorney Fanelli counseled the veterans to hold their parade away from the concert grounds, but they refused. Concert promoters too attempted to stop the parade with a court injunction—to no avail.

As the atmosphere of tension mounted, vacationers went back to their homes in New York. The anti-Semitism that had been simmering in Peekskill now flared into the open. The Jewish merchants who were left were terrorized, and some resort compounds organized twenty-four-hour-a-day guards.

Three days before the second concert, at a Civil Rights Congress rally in Harlem, Paul declared, "Yes, I will sing wherever the people want to hear me. I sing of peace and freedom and of life . . . If the State Troopers do not protect us, we shall have forces enough to protect ourselves." His gangster friend, Bumpy Johnson, offered his protection, but Paul gently refused it.

A note of warning about Peekskill's graver implications was sounded after the first concert in a published letter signed by twenty-three stage personalities. "A reenactment of the Nazi assault on culture and human life took place on the night of August 27 . . . This is a tragic moment for America, as it was a tragic moment sixteen years ago for Germany and the world." Among the signers: Oscar Hammerstein, Moss Hart, Henry Fonda, Uta Hagen, and Judy Holliday.[4]

On September 4, at 6:00 A.M., a private guard of 2,500 to 3,000 volunteers, mostly fur workers, longshoremen, and seamen, some of them armed with baseball bats, started to gather in Peekskill as they got off buses from New York.

About 11:00 A.M. the audience began to arrive by bus and car. Six hundred fifty newly deputized sheriffs and hundreds of state troopers showed up on the scene, lining the route of the parading legionnaires, who carried American flags and sang as they marched. A husky man who drove Paul to Peekskill said he was calmer than they. "He practiced his singing most of the way there," Harold Marcus recalled twenty-five years later.[5] Inside the country club grounds Paul's steps were determined as he stepped heavily onto the sound truck and walked to the microphone. Around him were fifteen men who formed a human wall between him and the hillside. The platform on which he stood sat beneath a giant oak tree, whose branches offered scant protection from the snipers some suspected of hiding in the thick trees beyond. Larry Brown, waiting for the familiar signal to begin, fixed him with a level gaze. The concert-goers—25,000 strong, including women, children, and even infants—sat on the grass beneath a bright, hot sun surrounded by a "Chinese Wall" of 2,500 guards. Above, on Redhill Road, more than a thousand protesters, held back by some 900 state troopers, hooted and jeered: "Reds!" "Jew Bastards!" "Go back to Russia!" "Nigger Lovers!" "Go back to Jew City!"

"This is my answer. I applaud you," Paul said. He clamped his right hand over his ear to drown out the chants and nodded to Larry to begin. His great voice ringing out over the hilltops of Peekskill, competing with buzzing helicopters that attempted to drown him out, Robeson sang several songs, including, "Go Down Moses," and some Negro work songs. In the last phrase of "Ol' Man River," he substituted for the original lines: "I must keep fightin' until I'm dyin'," as the crowd burst into applause.

Outside about 3,500 veterans and sympathizers marched and countermarched past the entrance, shouting epithets. The anti-Robeson mobs tried to attack late arrivals, and for a few minutes there was a free-for-all; several times the restless protestors tried to surge through police lines, but they were pushed back by husky troopers with nightsticks held chin high.

After the concert it was announced that no one would be permitted to leave until the way was cleared. Buses and cars were finally routed by the police up a steep, winding road through the woods. But toward Peekskill, strung out alongside Hillside Avenue for nearly two miles, demonstrators peppered the departing audience with rocks and stones. Hundreds of cars had windshields and windows shattered; eight were overturned and destroyed. In one incident, protestors dragged a woman from a car, took her baby from her, and threw her over a hedge.[6] Chartered buses from New York were pummeled by rocks, some the size of footballs, shattering windows; several drivers abandoned them. One man lost an eye; several arms were broken.

Peekskill Hospital was jammed as the injured began pouring in late Sunday afternoon, and New York hospitals reported that nearly fifty injured concert-goers drove all the way into the city before seeking medical care.

Newspaper accounts of the riot spoke of "anti-communists" and "communists and their sympathizers," although a majority of those attending the rally were not communists. The Peekskill *Evening Star* said the incident might bring "more good than harm," comparing the riots to the Boston Tea Party, which, it said, "was not in accordance with the then existing law but could not have been done in any other manner."[7] A more widespread reaction to the Peekskill violence called it a serious abridgement of constitutional guarantees of freedom of speech and assembly. Paul was furious and angrily demanded of

Dewey that he conduct an investigation. Essie called it "The Battle of Peekskill" and said, "today there is Civil War" in the United States.

Official investigators from the American Civil Liberties Union concluded that the Westchester County police permitted the assault upon the concert-goers, and that "the Communists did not provoke the disorders." Certain apologists for the violence, the report noted, insisted the concert-goers "provoked" the riot by simply exercising their constitutional right of free speech and free assembly, and by black men and white women riding in the same cars into the concert grounds.

Concluded the ACLU: "The determination to hold a peaceful assembly on private property, even by a hated minority, does not constitute provocation . . . From the evidence, one must conclude that the precipitating factors of the violence of September 4 lay within Peekskill itself."[8]

XVII:
Prisoner in
His Own Land

If Paul had "wondered what all the fuss was about" after Paris, he knew after Peekskill. On September 4 anti-black, anti-Semitic, and anti-communist forces had made him the focus of an epidemic of madness that was gripping the nation. The intensity had been building up all year. In March a man had been picked up in the middle of the night, running through the streets of Hobe Sound, Florida, screaming: "The Red Army has landed!"[1] It was former Secretary of Defense James V. Forrestal, who on May 22, died in an act of suicide that as one writer put it, "epitomized the anti-Red hysteria which gripped the land like some contagious psychosis at the time . . . "[2] All during the summer of 1949 newspapers, magazines, and military journals had daily carried forecasts and descriptions of the strategy of atomic warfare against the Soviet Union. In September, when President Truman announced that the Soviet Union had detonated an atomic device, hatred and fear reached a state of frenzy.

But the hysteria did not stop Paul from doing what he felt was right. After Peekskill he followed through on a promise to testify on behalf of eleven leaders of the communist party who were on trial. He spent five days waiting in the courtrooms and corridors. Finally, on September 21 he was called to the stand in the Federal Court House at Foley Square in New York City. Defense counsel, a diminutive black man named George W. Crockett, Jr., wanted Paul to testify that as one who had heard the defendants speak and read their writings, he felt they did not advocate the overthrow of the government by force and violence. But the district attorney objected to every one of Crockett's questions, and Judge Medina refused to let Paul address the court. "Mr. Robeson, I don't want to hear any statement from you," the judge insisted. "I can't find anything in these questions that you have any knowledge of the facts that are relevant in this case."

In late September the Council on African Affairs, saying that it "would not retreat," decided to go through with a series of concerts and meetings it had planned for Paul prior to Peekskill. It was a tense time; word was out that to hold a Paul Robeson concert meant to invite a riot. Louise Patterson, now an executive of the Council, was responsible for security and other details of the tour. There was harassment in every city, she recalled. In Detroit the Fire Department told the sponsoring group that they could not use single chairs, and a group of people had to spend the night before the concert wiring thousands of chairs together in rows. In Cincinnati and Akron intervention by the American Legion barred Paul from halls there. In Los Angeles opponents sponsored newspaper ads against his appearances. "Days and days before, we didn't even know if the concert was going to take place at all," said Mrs. Patterson. "You never knew if anybody was going to throw a bomb or not." Despite the many efforts made to stop the concert in Chicago, about 16,000 persons gathered in Wrigley Field.

The masses of black people, some of whom had been upset by Paul's reported Paris remarks, rallied around him on the tour, because Peekskill had provoked anger and outrage all over the country. "I think they were beginning to admire the guy's guts . . . by the way he thumbed his nose at people who could help him," recalled columnist Carl Rowan, who as a young reporter read avidly about Paul in those days. "What the people saw was that the loyalty Paul had was a bigger thing . . . Loyalty to the struggle . . . loyalty to the people . . . to the fight for freedom," said Louise Patterson.

Paul had asked that all of the policemen assigned to him be black whenever possible and in civilian clothes. "The way those men took care of Paul Robeson was simply beautiful," said Louise Patterson. "They would stand guard, some of them, all night long. And in every city it happened. Would Mr. Robeson autograph a program for their children? Did he have a picture that they could take home?"

At the end of the tour Paul returned to New York tired but glowing. He had aged a great deal during the six months since he had returned from Paris, and the strain of the tour told in his face, in his eyes, in loss of his easy stride. But there had been no riots, and blacks had rallied "like a homecoming." It gave him courage.

By now, Paul was under constant Federal Bureau of Investigation surveillance by agents who staked out his home and followed his movements. He said his telephone was wiretapped, so his friends were afraid to call, for fear of gathering thickening files of their own. Once J. Edgar Hoover decided Paul Robeson was "no good," he unleashed a whole range of FBI activities on him, all intended to deny him his First Amendment rights.

Paul was an easy target. After Peekskill the Soviet Government named a mountain in the Urals after him and perched a bust of him high at its peak. His address to the National Council of American Soviet Friendship at the Waldorf-Astoria was published early in 1950.

In Wheeling, West Virginia, on February 9, 1950, Senator Joseph McCarthy of Wisconsin stepped into the national spotlight holding his list of 205 alleged Communist party members "still working in the State Department and shaping policy." In Denver the next day he changed the term for his "subversives" from Communists to bad security risks, and in Salt Lake City he reconverted them to card-carrying Communists but reduced the number to fifty-seven. Despite the wavering, McCarthy made banner headlines and remained in the news almost without fail for more than four years.

Throughout that time Paul continued criticizing American policy. In March he attacked the State Department for barring a seventeen-member delegation from the World Peace Conference from entering the United States to present proposals for peace to President Truman. That same month Paul was asked, as co-chairman of the Progressive party, to appear with Congressman Adam Clayton Powell on Eleanor Roosevelt's NBC-TV show in a discussion of blacks in politics. After the idea was protested, NBC dropped it. Robeson did address a trade union conference on Negro rights in Chicago in early June; then, on June 25, 1950, the Korean war broke out.

According to the official version of events, it was a plain case of unprovoked aggression by the North Koreans, which could not have happened without the approval of the Soviet Union. Robeson, who had recently returned from Europe, had come back convinced otherwise. On June 28 at a mass rally of the Civil Rights Congress in New York City, Paul assailed United States intervention in Asia. He said at one point that troops ought to be sent to the South to fight the Klan instead of to Korea. A month later, police broke up a meeting of several thousand people assembled in New York's Union Square to hear Paul, W. E. B. Du Bois, and others talk against the war.

Paul had planned to travel to Eastern and Western Europe that summer, but he was soon to learn that the government had decided otherwise. On July 27 two agents of the State Department tried to reach Robeson at some friends' and said they wanted to ask him some questions. When they finally got in touch with him the next day, they demanded that he give up his passport. Paul refused. It didn't matter. A week later the State Department announced that Paul Robeson's passport had been canceled. Essie's and Pauli's passports too were to be revoked, though Essie refused to give hers up.

Paul was stunned by the State Department's action. He demanded to see Secretary of State Dean Acheson and have the government's conduct explained. He did not see Acheson. His passport had been canceled, he was told, because he refused to sign the noncommunist affiliation oath. He could get it back if he would sign a statement promising not to make any speeches when he was abroad. Robeson refused.

Newspapers took little interest in Paul's passport case, except to approve the State Department's actions. "Paul Robeson's record as an agitator . . . is well known. His plans call for an extensive series of appearances at European 'peace' rallies, followed by ideological traipsings through Africa and Australia . . . That is something this country can well be spared . . .," said the *New York Herald-Tribune* of August 6.

Even blacks tended to desert Paul at this time. Though many working-class blacks felt that white America had shut Paul up "the way they would like to shut up every black who thinks he has the same rights," the black middle class tended to run away from such controversial confrontation. To protect their jobs and their salaries they kept away from his concerts for fear of being tagged communist.

Except for leftists and some members of labor circles, most black leaders too stayed away from Paul. One snub, however, crushed him particularly. He was with an interracial group of friends in Small's Paradise in Harlem one day in the early fifties when he noticed Jackie Robinson and Don Newcombe across the room. Robeson sent a waiter to ask the baseball stars to come and meet his friends. "Fuck Paul Robeson," Jackie Robinson reportedly sneered. Dutifully, the embarrassed waiter relayed the message to Paul, who was dumbstruck. As Robinson and Newcombe left, Robinson brushed past, but

Newcombe lingered. "I apologize for him," Newcombe said. "He's sometimes that way."[3]

Because of his controversial beliefs, and his refusal to disavow them or his communist friends, Paul Robeson now found his countrymen both in and out of government treating him as a nonperson. After Peekskill, not only had more concert managers refused to book him, but suddenly his records were off the shelves in record shops. Books that listed him as a great American were removed from the shelves of libraries. An Enfield official wanted to bar him from Connecticut, and at Rutgers University, some alumni wanted to strike Paul's name from the college rolls and take back his academic degree and an honorary degree bestowed upon him in 1932. When the next American Sports Annual appeared, a mighty deletion had indeed occurred. For the years 1917 and 1918, when Paul had been named by Walter Camp as "All-American end," a blank space appeared; Paul Robeson's name had been left out. And Dr. Benjamin Mays refused to let a picture of Paul being granted an honorary degree some years earlier be published. He had recommended the honor for Robeson, he said, but the board wouldn't have accepted it had it been "after the general impression in this country that (Robeson) is affiliated in some way with the communistic movement. . . ."[4]

Renting halls to stage protest meetings became increasingly difficult. In the summer of 1950 Madison Square Garden refused to let the Council on African Affairs hold a Robeson passport rally because it was on the Attorney General's subversive list. In October Paul was forced to put up for sale the home in Enfield, Connecticut, which to Essie had always seemed the fulfillment of a dream.

Paul began to bring suit for restoration of his passport, a process that was to last for years. He maintained in court that not only did the Secretary of State have no authority to deny him the right to travel abroad, but that the laws requiring the noncommunist affidavit were unconstitutional. The State Department argued that a state of emergency existed, as declared by the President, and that the Secretary of State, in administering such emergency controls designed to safeguard the national security, clearly could decline to issue a passport to a present member of the Communist party. Meanwhile, Paul continued to apply for a passport as a "loyal, native-born American citizen." He tried to go to Paris in 1951 to place before the United Nations General Assembly a petition charging U.S. officials with acts against the Negro race that violated the Genocide Convention. The same year he applied for a passport to attend the International Peace Delegation in Paris and to attend a celebration of the second anniversary of the founding of the People's Republic of China. All were denied.

There was one bright new development. In 1951 Paul became the symbolic leader of the *Freedom* newspaper in Harlem. In turn, his fame as a radical cultural personality drew such Harlem writers as John Oliver Killens, twenty-year-old Lorraine Hansberry, and Julian R. Mayfield to the *Freedom* orbit, with an editorial board that included noted leftists, writer Shirley Graham Du Bois (the wife of W.E.B. Du Bois), the intellectual Louis E. Burnham, editor ("He taught me that *everything* is political," Lorraine said), and George B. Murphy, Jr., general manager. *Freedom* contained occasional reportorial pieces about Harlem schools and housing, but in the main, its writers hammered away at national and international issues—poll taxes, the Fair Employment Practices Commission, and the antilynch bill, China, British Guiana, the war in Korea, Africa. Paul himself wrote occasional articles about his passport ban and international affairs; his words in the October 1953 *Freedom* sound strangely familiar to contemporary ears. "No one has yet explained to my satisfaction what business a black lad from a Mississippi or Georgia share-cropping farm has in Asia shooting down the yellow or brown son of an impoverished rice farmer." All of this was perfectly in character for Paul, but in downplaying local issues in deference to the national and world scene, the paper became a curious anomaly—a Harlem paper that was not primarily about Harlem.

A conversation around a table at *Freedom* one day gives insight into Paul and Essie's relationship in these days. A group of people, including Louis Burnham, were talking with a black trade unionist who had just returned from the Soviet Union. The visitor was having trouble with his wife, and finally the conversation touched briefly on Paul and Essie, with Paul lashing out at one point, "Well, I just don't want to be in the house with her! And I don't want anybody worrying me about it." One intimate persisted, braving Paul's rage. "I don't think you ever have the right to discuss publicly in any way or to give anybody the impression that you are ever going to divorce Essie . . . I think it will hurt (our women) inside. Separation . . . no problem . . . but the two of you are intertwined in so many ways and life isn't over yet. I think that is a special burden and responsibility that you have to bear."[5]

In part, Paul and Essie's marriage was victimized by his career. His and Essie's unorthodox schedule in the early years made it a good idea for a family member to be with little Paul; Mrs. Goode, who had had an unhappy marriage, had a destructive influence on her daughter. One day in 1950 Essie tearfully confided in Marie Seton, who was staying with her at Enfield. "She broke down about the influence of her mother upon her . . . she realized now that her mother had been destructive in relation to Paul. It was true, Mrs. Goode and Essie had both been bossy, not only in relation to Paul but especially towards men who Paul liked being with. This really is what had gone wrong."[6]

For her part, Essie was in and out of the *Freedom* office, bringing in works of young artists, introducing them to Louis Burnham, asking him to give them a chance to write for the paper. She was there to welcome people from across the country and around the world, showing them the narrow rooms of the offices. In 1953 she was subpoenaed to appear at a Senate investigations subcommittee before Senator Joseph McCarthy. "I'm going to deal with this question of white supremacy," she confided to friends. Before the microphones and television cameras, the pillbox hat just so, she commented first on "how white the committee was" and how she didn't know what a communist cell was. Commented McCarthy later: "She appears to be charming." In Cleveland soon after, an elevator operator stopped Essie. "You know I saw you on that TV and you were beautiful. And you sure looked fine." Praise from such poles convinced Essie that she had been the kind of representative of her people that she wished to be, a friend commented.

Robeson was now constantly shadowed by the FBI, and a man long accustomed to walking proudly found himself sometimes slipping stealthily through doors and bounding up stairways. He became adept at recognizing plainsclothesmen. His lifestyle was more gypsylike as well, friends said. He lived part of the time with his brother, Ben, intermittently with Essie, at other times with various friends or in his own apartment alone. It was in this atmosphere that several young budding actors and entertainers, some of whom would later become black superstars—Sidney Poitier, Harry Belafonte, Ossie Davis, Leon Bibb, and Julian Mayfield—got it into their heads that Paul needed protection, and they started accompanying him.

"We didn't want him walking around by himself," recalled Julian Mayfield a quarter-century later. "We loved Paul. Why? Because white people hated him so. We just wanted to be around him. It was a question of choosing sides and we chose Robeson . . . His brother Ben had two or three beautiful daughters, and we were all young men and there we were . . . "[7]

Paul looked upon Poitier and Mayfield as young men of the theater, and they would ask him somewhat awed questions: "What was it like in the Soviet Union?" "How did you really feel playing the Great Moor?" Walking around Harlem with Paul, they would come across wizened men and balloon-cheeked youngsters shooting craps or gulping from a bottle who would suddenly look up in wonder. "Ain't that Paul?" "Is that Mr. Robeson?" Paul would stride purposefully forward to shake their hands, prompting a shake of a battered head or a starlike gaze. How could anybody who had been so big risk all of that to go against The Man?

Once, when Paul was staying with a white family off Central Park West, Sidney and Julian called for him and took him in a taxi up to Julian's little apartment where they talked to him about their problems, asking if they should marry their girlfriends. "He told us all these stories and at the end of the evening we didn't know where he stood . . . Much of the time he was serious," Mayfield recalled. "But when he laughed, he made the room shake. He was angry because I think he did not understand how he could have been the golden boy all those years and then they turned on him."

The "great wells of happiness, great wells of sadness" that Paul, Jr., described in his father were never more evident than during these blacklist days. Ollie Harrington, contributing cartoonist at *Freedom*, recalled Paul's buoyancy during a session of "talkin' and signifyin'." On one occasion, Paul, sitting astride his old desk in the tiny office, was beguiling Lou Burnham, George Murphy, and a secretary on the wizardry of old Josh Gibson, Satchel Paige, and other black players jimcrowed out of baseball. "One day our boys are going to bust right into the Yankee Stadium dugout and teach 'em the fine points of the game." The petite secretary's eyes twinkled as she asked, "Mister Robeson, shall I make a note to get a committee together this afternoon?" Harrington recalled that Paul "stopped in midsentence and then 'fell out.' Lou dissolved into a laughter-shaken mass on a pile of newspapers, and George, always cool, sat shaking his head. The secretary was Lorraine Hansberry."

These were the years of extremely hard exile from the concert stage and commercial theater. With the long and expensive legal battle to regain his passport, Robeson seemed to age before his friends' eyes. "To a man with his tremendous energy and creativity, it was a terrible period," said Louise Patterson. In some respects, it was "worse . . .

than being in prison." She used to visit him when he was living with his brother in the parish house, next to Mother A.M.E. Zion Church, where Ben pastored. "He was in a little room and he would sit up there with his records."

Paul was still determined to sing. He sang in parks and high school auditoriums. But it was especially in the churches that Robeson found much of his audience during these lean years, as he returned to sing in its place of origin the music of his people. He and Larry Brown performed at the Peace Arch Park on the United States-Canadian border in a concert sponsored by the International Union of the Mine, Mill and Smelter Workers, when he was denied entry into Canada, on May 18, 1952. Before singing he told the 40,000 men, women, and children gathered on that sunny Sunday:

> I stand here today under great stress because I dared, as do all of you, to fight for peace and a decent life for all men, women and children wherever they may be. And especially today I stand fighting for the rights of my people in this America in which I was born. You have known me through many years. I am the same Paul, fighting a little harder because the times call for harder struggle. This historic occasion probably means that I shall be able to sing again as I want to . . . to sing freely without being stopped here and there . . .

But his prediction proved premature. Two years later he was again stopped at the Canadian border and was forced a second time to conduct the concert at the border.

In 1952 Paul was awarded the Lenin Peace Prize "for promotion of Peace among nations." U.N. correspondent James Hicks recalled he was the only reporter who sought him out for an interview. "When I finished work that day, I was tailed home to my place in Brooklyn. As I pulled in that night after completing my work I'll be damned if a car did not pull up alongside of my little old Ford. It turned out to be two agents from the FBI. They said, 'You interviewed Robeson today, didn't you?' I said, 'Yes.' It's fantastic when you look at it today."

In 1953 Robeson sought to travel to Europe to participate in an artistic production. Again the Passport Division denied him that right, saying he really wanted to go to Russia to accept his peace award. In July 1954 he asked permission to "sing and act" in England, Israel, and possibly France and the Soviet Union, but all these requests were denied on grounds that Robeson consistently refused to submit the affidavit regarding his relationship to the world communist movement.

Meanwhile, the Korean war droned on, feeding the continuing McCarthy hysteria, until by the end of 1954 two events, on opposite sides of the same coin, in a sense, marked the end of an era. The American Communist party was outlawed, and the Senate censured Senator Joseph McCarthy in a motion on December 2, 1954, ending his reign of terror. For some blacks the official end of the Communist party in the United States was something of an anticlimax. Earlier in the year the famous *Brown* vs. *the Board of Education* decision by the Supreme Court changed the political alignment of many Negro leftists. The victory catapulted the NAACP to new heights and pushed the Supreme Court into a new social revolutionary role. In the post-*Brown* euphoria, many among the Communist party's small black constituency abandoned the party.

One of the victims of this realignment was *Freedom*, which would succumb by the July-August 1955 issue. Harold Cruse, in *The Crisis of the Negro Intellectual*, was especially critical of what he felt was Paul's inability to make his message in *Freedom* relevant to the bulk of Harlemites. *Freedom*, wrote Cruse, was no more than a Negro version of the Communist *Daily Worker*.

> *What Killens, Robeson, and their middle-class leftwing ethos truly idealized were nice, upright Negro workers, who, even if they did go to church and worship God and not Russia, at least tilled the Southern soil as solid citizen sharecroppers, or worked in factories or service industries but were never, never anti-union; who always knew which American wars were progressive and which were "imperialistic;" who instinctively loved all foreign-born whites and were never, never anti-Semitic, and (God forbid!) who never, but never had a single nationalistic sentiment in their naive revolutionary souls!*

Between the constant legal bouts for his passport, Paul continued his work with the Council on African Affairs. The importance of the Council, now that organizations on Africa are numerous, is easy to overlook. It was barely known outside of the East Coast, and it was never a mass-based group. But the Council of the 1930s and 1940s was a pioneer in bringing the question of Africa, and the fight against colonialism to the consciousness of people in America. Nevertheless, in June 1955 Paul was forced to preside over the group's disbanding. The executive board of the Council on African Affairs had decided to terminate activities because "continuing Government harassment" made their work impossible. This first predominantly black organization dedicated to African liberation from colonialism through attempts to influence U.S. policies was dead. It was one of the saddest days in Paul's life. He had been a man, he said, living on top of a mountain, who had now descended into the valley.

XVIII: "Are You Now...?"

Paul's name had intermittently emerged in connection with so-called subversive activities in hearings and investigations for years, from Congressman Martin Dies's questioning of Robeson's role in the prolabor play *Stevedore* in 1938, to the post-1946 period, when his name was cropping up regularly before various investigating committees. Much of the time he was named in the testimony of so-called "friendly" witnesses from right-wing organizations. For example, Walter S. Steele, chairman of the National Security Committee of the American Coalition of Patriotic, Civic and Fraternal Societies, named Paul dozens of times in his sweeping testimony of July 21, 1947, letting drop with deadly offhand casualness such statements as Paul's having "eighty radical connections." So synonymous had his name become with treason that one witness, Adolph Menjou, who was asked when an American's patriotism might be questioned, answered, "if he owns Paul Robeson records."

Although the House Un-American Activities Committee's investigations figured in the retraction of Paul's passport in August 1950, it was not until 1956 that Paul was actually called to testify before the group. It is of considerable irony that by this year, his period of professional exile had begun slowly to draw to an end. Robeson had been elated in February when he finally received permission to travel as far as Canada, and he received a standing ovation in Toronto. By now he was fifty-eight, and the stress of blacklisting had taken its physical toll; he looked a little frail by comparison to his usual massive self. But in Toronto he had stood erect and proudly on the concert stage, cupping his right hand over his right ear, as he sang twenty-one songs. Then he read a scene from *Othello* and recited lines from Chilean poet Pablo Neruda's defiant "Let the Rail Splitter Awake."

It was a rough year for Paul and Essie. Many of their goods were still in packing crates—they had moved several times before settling at 16 Jumel Terrace in Harlem. Then, he was subpoenaed to testify before a HUAC subcommittee. He arrived in Washington the night before and his friend George Murphy got him settled into a hotel. Murphy did not attend the session, however.

The date was June 12, 1956. As Paul and his counsel, Milton H. Friedman, entered the Old House Office Building the day was pleasantly warm, even a faint breeze stirred, and that was not always the case on a June day in Washington although the flowers bloomed brightly on Capitol Hill. By mid-afternoon, the sun would be a fiery ball and the temperature near 90°, and the tempers Paul Robeson would leave behind would be scorching too. Uncharacteristically, Paul was early for the 10:00 A.M. session.

Chairman Francis E. Walter convened the Committee on Un-American Activities subcommittee in the caucus room. Seated with Representative Walter were his colleagues, Representatives Clyde Doyle of California, Bernard W. Kearney of New York, and Gordon H. Scherer of Ohio.

The chairman called the committee to order, announced that the hearing was on the use of U.S. passports as travel documents "in furtherance of the objectives of the Communist conspiracy."(Two weeks earlier, New Hampshire churchman Willard Uphaus appeared before Walter and four years later he was behind bars. Nine days after Paul appeared, playwright Arthur Miller faced the Inquisitors. He was sentenced to jail but acquitted on appeal.)

Paul Robeson's mobile face was expressionless as he walked forward to the witness chair, but by the time he had identified himself he felt his anger rising over what the tribunal now represented—a hideous bulldozer crushing reputations, professional standings, marriages, careers in its wake. And within minutes, the beads of perspiration had popped onto his massive face.

After a few preliminaries, the questioning was begun by subcommittee Counsel Richard Arens.

Mr. Arens: "Are you now a member of the Communist Party?"

Mr. Robeson: "Oh, please, please, please."

Rep. Scherer: "Please answer, will you, Mr. Robeson?"

Mr. Robeson: "What is the Communist Party? What do you mean by that?"

Mr. Scherer: "I ask that you direct the witness to answer the question."

June 12, 1956: Robeson before the House Un-American Activities Committee in Washington, D.C.

Mr. Robeson: "What do you mean by the Communist Party? As far as I know, it is a legal party like the Republican Party and the Democratic Party. Do you mean—which, belonging to a party of Communists or belonging to a party of people who have sacrificed for my people and for all Americans and workers, that they can live in dignity? Do you mean that party?"

Mr. Arens: "Are you now a member of the Communist Party?"

Mr. Robeson: "Would you like to come to the ballot box when I vote and take out the ballot and see?"

Mr. Arens: "Mr. Chairman, I respectfully suggest that the witness be ordered and directed to answer that question."

The Chairman: "You are directed to answer the question."

Mr. Robeson: "I stand upon the Fifth Amendment."

Mr. Scherer: "I did not hear the answer."

Mr. Robeson: "I stand upon the Fifth Amendment of the American Constitution."

Mr. Arens: "Do you mean you invoke the Fifth Amendment?"

Mr. Robeson: "I invoke the Fifth Amendment."

Mr. Arens: "Do you honestly apprehend that if you told this committee truthfully whether or not you are presently . . ."

Mr. Robeson: "I have no desire to consider anything. I invoke the Fifth Amendment and it is none of your business what I would like to do and I invoke the Fifth Amendment. And forget it."

The Chairman: "You are directed to answer that question."

Mr. Robeson: "I invoke the Fifth Amendment and so I am not answering. I am answering it, am I not?"

Mr. Arens: "I respectfully suggest the witness be ordered and directed to answer the question as to whether or not he honestly apprehends, that if he gave us a truthful answer to this last principal question, he would be supplying information which might be used against him in a criminal proceeding."

The Chairman: "You are directed to answer that question, Mr. Robeson."

Mr. Robeson: "Gentlemen, in the first place, wherever I have been in the world and I have been in many places, Scandinavia, England and many places, the first to die in the struggle against Fascism were the Communists and I laid many wreaths upon graves of Communists. It is not criminal and the Fifth Amendment has nothing to do with criminality. The Chief Justice of the Supreme Court, Warren, has been very clear on that in many speeches that the Fifth Amendment does not have anything to do with the inference of criminality. I invoke the Fifth Amendment."

Arens then called out the names of several individuals who were allegedly involved in a communist conspiracy and asked Paul if he knew them. At one point Paul laughed out loud, prompting Representative Scherer to snap that it was not a laughing matter. "It is to me. This is really complete nonsense," said Paul.

Paul characterized Chairman Walter, author of the controversial McCarran-Walter Immigration Act, as "the author of bills that are going to keep all kinds of decent people out of the country."

"No, "Walter retorted, "only your kind."

"Colored people like myself, from the West Indies and all kinds. You don't want any colored people. You want to shut up every Negro who stands up for his rights."

"We are trying," said Walter, "to make it easier to get rid of your kind, too."

The session grew stormier; Paul explained what he said in Paris in 1949 and why, declaring again and again that his motivations were concern for the freedom of black Americans and for the liberation of Africa. Yes, he did love the Soviet people and he sent Paul, Jr., to school there, but he was not part of a conspiracy to overthrow the government of the United States, he testified.

Mr. Scherer: "You are here because you are promoting the Communist cause."

Mr. Robeson: "I am here because I am opposing the neo-Fascist cause which I see arising in these committees. You are like the Alien [and] Sedition Act, and Jefferson could be sitting here, and Frederick Douglass could be sitting here, and Eugene Debs could be here."

Questioned about his son's Russian schooling, Paul said, "He suffered no prejudice like he would here in Washington."

The Chairman: "Now what prejudice are you talking about? You were graduated from Rutgers and you were graduated from the University of Pennsylvania.[1] I remember seeing you play football at Lehigh."

Mr. Robeson: "We beat Lehigh."

The Chairman: "And we had a lot of trouble with you."

Mr. Robeson: "That is right. De Wysocki was playing in my team."

The Chairman: "There was no prejudice against you. Why did you not send your son to Rutgers?"[2]

Mr. Robeson: "Just a moment. It all depends a great deal. This is something that I challenge very deeply, and very sincerely, the fact that the success of a few Negroes, including myself or Jackie Robinson can make up—and here is a study from Columbia University—for $700 a year for thousands of Negro families in the South. My father was a slave and I have cousins who are sharecroppers and I do not see my success in terms of myself. That is the reason, my own success has not meant what it should mean. I have sacrificed literally hundreds of thousands, if not millions, of dollars for what I believe in."

The questioning continued in that vein for some time. Walter was incredulous when Paul called communist leader Ben Davis "patriotic" and "one of my dearest friends." During the hearing Paul tried unsuccessfully to read a statement into the record. "Tell us what Communists helped you to prepare it," Arens asked contemptuously. (Paul's statement charged the government with trying to "gag me here and abroad" and said that Secretary of State Dulles was "afraid" to let him have a passport because of his "recognized status as a spokesman for large sections of Negro Americans" and because he had "been for years extremely active in behalf of independence of colonial peoples of Africa." But the main reason for the cancellation of the passport, he felt, was Dulles's objections to his speaking abroad "against the oppression suffered by my people in the United States . . . I am proud that those statements can be made about me . . ." Robeson would have concluded.)

Finally the Chairman declared: "Just a minute, the hearing is now adjourned."
Mr. Robeson: "I should think it would be."
The Chairman: "I have endured all of this that I can stand."

Walter's banging gavel adjourned the hearing, and the subcommittee voted to seek contempt action against Paul because of his "entire conduct" during the hearing, his personal attacks on the committee, and his "smear" of a senator. The "smear" was a reference to Paul's remark that it would be "unthinkable that any people would take up arms in the name of an Eastland." (James Eastland was chairman of the Senate Judiciary Committee and an outspoken foe of the Supreme Court's school integration ruling.) The contempt action was never taken.

Paul's passport case was still undecided. It was one of several that had been brought into the federal courts to challenge the power of the Passport Office of the State Department to decide whether an applicant should be permitted to travel. The State Department's brief, which had been submitted to the Court of Appeals in February 1952, contained an interesting statement in opposition to Paul's claim of his right to a passport:

> Futhermore, even if the complaint had alleged, which it does not, that the passport was cancelled solely because of the applicant's recognized status as spokesman for large sections of Negro Americans, we submit that this would not amount to an abuse of discretion in view of appellant's frank admission that he has been for years extremely active politically in behalf of independence of the colonial peoples of Africa.

Three months after his subcommittee appearance in Washington, Paul requested that the Supreme Court intervene in his right-to-travel case. But in November the Supreme Court upheld a lower court ruling and rejected Paul's appeal.

The international pressure to give Paul passport privileges had been building steadily for years. It too was reaching a climax. In January 1957 *Pravda* broadcast a message of greeting from him. The same year Actors' Equity in Britain urged the American Equity Council to help fight for his passport.

A few months later, still unable to get a passport, Paul sang and spoke for twenty-three minutes via telephone to an audience of 1,000 in London. In that instance American Telephone and Telegraph helped Paul make the State Department look a little silly. In the fall he again used the coaxial cable beneath the Atlantic, this time to sing for the miners of Wales at the traditional Welsh cultural festival, Eisteddfod.

Significantly, the October 1957 issue of *Ebony* magazine ran an article entitled "Has Paul Robeson Betrayed the Negro?" by Carl T. Rowan, then a Minneapolis reporter who had proposed the story to publisher John H. Johnson. "In the context of the times, it was a courageous thing for Johnson to do," Rowan recalled nearly twenty years later. The article told the facts on both sides, including Paul's hesitancy to criticize the Soviet Union even when such criticism was deserved. "I think the Negro should solve his problems within the American framework . . . But he never will achieve integration until the time comes when all Negroes show complete solidarity, backed by all the colored people of the world," Paul concluded to Rowan.

Paul seemed to receive a grim satisfaction from thumbing his nose at the State Department in a public way. Privately, however, he was growing increasingly angry—bitter and restive. People who met him were struck by his resistance to any humor or effort at warmth. "He seemed to be intense all of the time, driven, and I attribute it to a profound frustration," recalled Stanley Levinson, an associate in Othello Associates, a small venture formed to produce several of his recordings during the blacklist period.

It was during this period that Paul, with the help of his longtime friend Lloyd L. Brown, an editor of *Masses and Mainstream*, began writing a book—addressed primarily to black Americans—to explain what he had done and why. Most of the white American press in America was silent on *Here I Stand*, when it was published in 1958, continuing the ban against mentioning Paul (except for references to him as a "left-wing singer" or "procommunist") that had been set in motion in 1950. The foreign press gave the book critical acclaim, as did many black newspapers. The Baltimore *Afro-American* serialized several chapters and featured a review by Saunders Redding, the noted historian, who later listed the work among the ten that most impressed him during the year. Only the NAACP magazine, *Crisis*, dissented, finding the book "disorderly and confusing," and calling Robeson a man whom "Negroes . . .never regarded as a leader," and who "imagines his misfortunes to stem, not from his own bungling, but from the persecution of the 'white folks on top.'" Yet even that review, by bringing Paul's plight before the public, acted as yet another voice in the growing chorus calling for restoration of Paul's freedom to travel.

In the fall of 1957 Paul gave successful concerts in Canada and on the West Coast. His militancy had not changed, but times had. The American people were growing up, Paul felt, and his new manager, Paul Endicott, echoed this by saying Paul was breaking through to the newly grown-up public, "the kind of audience you want." One of these audiences, for example, was at a celebration of Negro History Week in Oakland, California. Paul did not abandon "politicking" during his concerts, but more and more he did it through his music. For example, he added to his recitals part of the Hymn to Joy of Beethoven's Ninth Symphony, singing the line "All men are brothers" with particular pathos. He'd been fighting all of his life to prove that statement; he'd sacrificed hundreds of thousands of dollars, his time, talent and emotional life for it. "I intend to continue fighting to prove it the rest of my life," he said.

In April of 1958 Paul was finally permitted to travel in the western hemisphere where no passport was required. The following month, on May 9, he gave his first Carnegie Hall recital in eleven years and was greeted by a long standing ovation. The emotion of the occasion

Robeson with his passport after a 1958 Supreme Court decision restored his right to travel abroad

seemed to infuse new life into Paul, now sixty, and he looked better than he had in years. He thrust out his arms and spread his fingers as he sang, seeming to merge his being into complete identification with the music. One could almost feel the tension drain from his body, as his clear bass boomed in the great concert hall. The critics marveled that he could hold the attention of his audience by the force of his personality, bringing the group to its feet at the end in a standing ovation.

Because the churches, gigantic and tiny, had opened their doors to Paul when concert halls like Carnegie locked theirs, Paul felt a special love and obligation to them. And so it was not at Carnegie, but at his brother Ben's Mother A.M.E. Zion Church in Harlem that one of the most special concerts of his comeback occurred. It was the same church where he sometimes sat in the balcony during the long years of exile, inspiring, someone said years later, countless little choir members to go home, preen before their mirrors, and pretend they were Paul Robeson. In this concert more than any other, his songs spoke for his politics. He sang "Swing Low, Sweet Chariot," and "No More Auction Block." The crowd hung breathlessly on the emotion of the words. He went on to sing, "The house I live in . . . the people I meet, all races, all religions that's America to me. . . . " They interrupted him to burst into applause. And when he told them, "I want the folks of Mother Zion to know that a lot of hard struggle is over and that my concert career has practically been reestablished all over the country . . . This could not have happened without the strength and the courage and the help and the prayers of you not only here in Mother Zion but also in many parts of America . . . I hope soon that it will be possible to travel all over the world to accept many invitations. . . . " The clapping thundered into the street.

The next month, in June 1958, the Supreme Court ruled that the State Department had no right under law to deny a passport because of a person's "beliefs and associations." On June 27 Paul received his passport and the right to travel abroad. The offers that had been coming regularly through the years from all over the world now deluged him. But he had decided to go to England, and on July 12, he and Essie were in London. Paul was finally a free man.

XIX:
Free at Last

Paul displayed the old charisma as he appeared on British television soon after his arrival in England. His expressiveness seemed intensified; he was relaxed and happy. In July he sang in Royal Albert Hall, his first concert abroad in eight years, and the audience, jammed into the auditorium for his return appearance, went wild.

Harry Belafonte opened the same night in London and the reporters rushed over afterward to catch Belafonte's last numbers. Backstage, one asked the performer why his show had so much humor, while Paul had evidenced none. "It is because of the price Mr. Robeson paid that I can afford to have a sense of humor," Belafonte replied.[1]

The day after the concert Paul visited Hy Kraft, who had written the script for the all-black movie, *Stormy Weather*, and also the book for the Broadway hit, *Top Banana*. Kraft, a great admirer of Paul's since the 1920s, had said, "When he shakes your hand, a transfusion takes place." Kraft, too, had been blacklisted and was living in London. "We talked for a couple of hours and then we walked a few blocks," Kraft recalled years later. "Strangers greeted him. It wasn't like that in his own country. Then he hailed a cab. As Paul got in he called the driver's attention to the fact that he hadn't dropped the meter flag. The driver said, 'It's an honor to have you, Mr. Robeson. It's my pleasure.'"[2]

But Paul longed to return to the Soviet Union. In August he went to Moscow for his first concert appearance there in nine years. The Russian people welcomed him and Essie as old and dear friends, and Paul was hailed as a hero, a fighter for the colored peoples of the world. In the fall the couple vacationed at a Crimean resort and had a "friendly and cordial" talk with Premier Nikita Khrushchev. Paul stayed on holiday almost a month, performing at a nearby children's camp.

"It is impossible," said Konstantin Kudrov, a journalist acquaintance, who briefly had been Paul's interpreter in 1934 and 1937, "to describe the enthusiastic welcome . . . at Artek. He was asked to repeat a song five times."[3] At a hastily arranged get-together in Primorsky Park in Yalta on September 6, Paul was feted with speeches and later sang songs of black people, British, Russians, and Uzbeks. "I can still hear that wonderful duet (with Ivan Kozlovsky, former leading tenor of the Bolshoi Company)."[4] Robeson was proud of his friendship for the Soviet people; he still felt that Russia's history made it clear that it would be the friend of colonial peoples struggling for liberation in the future.

In September Paul and Essie returned to England, with an announcement that he would make his future home there. London would be his center, as Hollywood was the center for some British filmstars. Yet he insisted, "I don't want any overtones of suggestions that I am deserting America."

He went on tour in England and in November became the first black person to stand at the lectern of St. Paul's Cathedral. Four thousand persons were seated inside, and another 5,000 waited outside while he sang. As he left, he was mobbed by well-wishers and had to be rescued by police.

Already in 1958 Robeson had to cancel concerts because of bad health, but 1959 saw the beginning of the illnesses that would plague him the rest of his life. "Any illness he later suffered I lay at the door of those years of house arrest," Louise Patterson would say in 1974. In any case, it cast a shadow over his newly restored freedom. In mid-December Paul and Essie returned to Moscow for a month, but illness forced him into a Kremlin hospital in early January 1959. Hospitalized for treatment of influenza and tests for dizziness, he was almost forced to cancel completely a role he dearly wanted to play. He had been scheduled to play *Othello* once again, this time at Stratford-on-Avon, in a production by Glen Bynam Shaw. When he emerged from the hospital and went off to the Black Sea to recuperate, the doctors said "absolutely not" to any idea of his exerting himself on the stage. The physical and nervous strain of the long years of exile had taken their toll. Deeply disappointed, Essie wrote Shaw that Paul would have to cancel his commitment.

But Paul progressed well, and his doctors finally decided that he could go through with the production if he relied on his voice and kept his physical activity to a minimum, and cut down on the number of

A visit with Nikita Khrushchev in the Crimea, Russia, August 1958

performances. News that Robeson *would* appear resulted in sell-out performances.

The Robesons arrived back in England in March to begin rehearsals for *Othello,* a job Paul considered the toughest of his career. Because they had lost much rehearsal time, director Tony Richardson put Robeson through the play twice daily, often working until midnight. The production, which included Sam Wanamaker as Iago, Mary Ure as Desdemona, and Albert Finney as Cassio, opened the hundredth season of the Stratford Memorial Theatre, just two days before his sixty-first birthday. The final curtain was raised fifteen times to please first-nighters.

The verdicts were good for Paul; in fact, some critics thought his maturity gave him more confidence and authority in the role. But the production itself fared less well, judged too fast-paced, "fussy" even. It didn't matter. Playing at Stratford had fulfilled one of Robeson's theatrical ambitions, and the production was a landmark for him.

But it was as if *Othello* were only an interlude. Increasing strain and fatigue dogged him, even as he toured the British Isles again and sang to favorable notices and adoring crowds. The accoutrements of age, such as eyeglasses to read his notes, notwithstanding, Robeson held audiences in his absolute sway. It was the intimacy of contact that made his recitals so different—the sense of spontaneity and improvisation as he riffled about in papers on the piano and chatted with Lawrence Brown. Paul's message, his social concern, was ever present. He seemed almost to feel that a concert was not worthwhile if the audience did not share his passionate concern for the equality of all men.

In 1960 Paul made what was to be his final major concert tour, going to Australia and New Zealand. To the recurring question of whether he could sing at sixty-two, reviewers gave a resounding "yes!" Louise Patterson, who visited the Robesons in London after the tour, recalled, "Paul was in great spirits after the reception he'd had in Australia. And of course he never knew how to spare himself. Wherever he was asked to go, he went, and I guess it was right after that—a few months after that he became ill . . . I think probably having overdone himself with all these tours. He was gone three weeks, and I think he was going every minute of the time—big concerts; a group of workers wanted him here . . . everywhere. And after sitting for eight years . . . "

That year Paul received the German Peace Medal from the German

Paul Robeson and Mary Ure rehearse *Othello* at Stratford-on-Avon, England, April 1959

Democratic Republic. Professor Albert Norden, a member of the Central Committee of the Socialist Unity Party, said on that occasion, "You and I are privileged to witness and help in that epoch-making movement of liberation of the African people who are now entering the great community of the United Nations."

And the same day, in East Berlin, Paul was given an honorary doctorate of philosophy by Humboldt University. The *Laudatie* read: "He is to be thanked that innumerable revolutionary songs, Worker and Negro Songs, the music of simple people have been preserved for coming generations. Above all he is to be thanked for making world famous the true, fighting character of Negro music." Smiling broadly, though the lines in his face were etched deeply and showed the strains of illness, Paul thanked his listeners "for your help over the years of tremendous struggle and persecution . . . I came as a sort of student, like you all . . . I think I am what you would call an eternal student. And here I leave you as a doctor."

During those frequent visits to East Germany, Paul spent a good deal of time with his friend Oliver (Ollie) Harrington, the painter-cartoonist whose famous "Bootsie" cartoons appeared in a number of black newspapers, and his East German wife.

Harrington felt Robeson's "imprisonment" had made him distrustful of his American friends—many white liberals had left him out of fear, as did some blacks he knew—but he was constantly supported by the Soviet Union and other Socialist countries. Thus Paul felt he could trust the Russians, and continued to go to Russia to be treated for his illnesses.

Robeson seemed to be a hero in East Germany for psychological as well as ideological reasons. There were still guilt feelings among the Germans about the Jewish extermination during World War II. In trying to turn its back on racism and anti-Semitism and to demonstrate this new beginning, the East Germans embraced black heroes, and particularly Robeson.

Paul again fell ill in 1961, and he did not sing in a full public concert again. Instead, he spent the next three years in Europe, in and out of hospitals, sanitariums, and nursing homes, in London, Moscow, and the German Democratic Republic.

Mrs. Alphaeus Hunton saw Paul in Russia in 1962. "He had suffered a nervous breakdown," Mrs. Hunton recalled. "He went to the Soviet Union for treatment. They had him in a sanitarium, and Alphaeus and I went, and I'll never forget this. He was sitting in a room all alone, and he was so depressed . . . terribly depressed. And they wouldn't let anybody see him, well naturally. But he was so delighted to see Alphaeus, he got up and he put his arms around him and then the two of them went out in the garden and strolled around for maybe a half hour or so and the change that came over him during that short period of time—being with someone you like and love and had worked with for that many years. He was sort of isolated. Oh, they meant the best in the world for him but he was away from people . . . away from his own people and people who really *knew* him. And it did a lot to cheer him up and make him feel so much better."

Robeson's breakdown was physical, reliable sources say, due to cerebral vascular disorders. Essie felt that what he needed most was "an extended rest and quiet to make up for all the years of work, pressure and tension to which he has been subjected. More than 35 years of it." But by now Essie, too, was intermittently ill. According to George Murphy, a close family friend, she suffered from cancer and later had a breast removed. Yet she successfully sheltered Paul from the press.

Around 1963 rumors began appearing in the American and British press, and headlines appeared in some papers in Europe, that Paul had become a bitter man, disenchanted with Russian communism. No statement or retraction was ever offered. Perhaps none should have been expected. But by then Paul *was* a broken man—broken by the strain of an eight-year period of deprivation.

Later in 1963 as his health improved somewhat, Paul left Moscow and spent time convalescing in East Berlin. It was time to come home, and he returned to America by way of London. He was thrilled at the prospect of seeing Paul, Jr., Marilyn, and his two grandchildren, David and Susan, whom he had not seen for five years. The Robesons also needed the care of their family. Paul and Essie arrived in New York City on December 23. They were coming home to be among their people, their family, and their friends for the first time since July 1958. The press met them at the airport, and a reporter badgered Paul with questions. "Is it true you're disillusioned with communism?" Essie snapped back, "He thinks communism is terrific." It was an unfriendly answer to an unfriendly question, a reminder of the past for the man who was now thin and frail, if erect and smiling, with his eyes hidden behind his heavy glasses.

Active participation was now a thing of the past for Paul. He and Essie returned to Jumel Terrace in Harlem and lived quietly. With their

Paul Robeson, greeted by his son, as he returns to the United States from a 5-year, self-imposed exile, December 1963

savings and his royalties, they could have chosen to live on Park Avenue, where Paul had been briefly in the 1940s, but Harlem was his homeground. His love for his people had always governed his life, and he wanted to spend these last years among his own.

His physical decline continued. One day Dorothy and Alphaeus Hunton went up to Jumel Terrace to see him. "His physical condition was deteriorating and at that time, well, it was a sad thing to see Paul," Mrs. Hunton remembered.

He emerged from seclusion for public appearances only rarely. "We're moving!" he exclaimed exultantly in his last public statement— on the first anniversary of the 1963 March on Washington. On September 2, 1964, he spoke at the funeral of his friend Benjamin J. Davis, Jr., the communist leader, in Harlem. In April 1965, 2,500 friends and admirers gathered at the Hotel Americana to pay him tribute in a four-hour presentation arranged by *Freedomways* magazine, introduced by Ossie Davis. The *Amsterdam News* said Paul "bounded up the stairs like a panther, his massive figure just slightly stooped." Robeson also appeared in public to honor the memory of his young friend, Lorraine Hansberry. But by late 1965 the serious breakdown of his health sidelined him permanently, and he retired from public life.

On December 13, 1965, Essie finally succumbed at New York's Beth Israel Hospital to the cancer that had plagued her later years. She was sixty-eight. Theirs had been an erratic and, for both of them, at times an emotionally difficult relationship. "Without her I would never have achieved what I did," Paul had said many times. She had shared his politics and labors on behalf of Africans and for black Americans, and they both believed deeply in the equality of all men. She had loyally defended Paul during the blacklist days, attacking both black and white critics of his positions on his behalf. And she had Paul's deep gratitude for her help and guidance over those many years of struggle and achievement. When she died, Paul was more alone than at any time since the death of his father. With Essie gone, he needed constant care and attention. He moved to a twelve-room house in a middle-income black neighborhood in Philadelphia, the home of his older sister, Mrs. Marion Forsythe, who had by then retired from a teaching career. With his son to look after his affairs, Paul was sustained and comforted by his family. For a handful of closest friends—Dr. Sam Rosen and his wife, Helen, black writer Lloyd L. Brown—the door would swing open when Paul felt well enough to receive them. Occasionally, friends such as the Reverend Aaron Hoggard, pastor of the St. James A.M.E. Zion

Church, would pray with Paul or take him out for automobile rides. He passed the time reading and occasionally went out to a show like *Hello Dolly*, which starred Pearl Bailey.

Casual visitors, newsmen, all but the most intimate of friends found the blinds of the two-story row house drawn, even in the middle of the day. Opening the door by no more than an inch, Mrs. Forsythe would tell a caller that it was nice of them to call, and that her brother would be heartened, but that he would see no one. A sadness, even a keen regret, not bitterness, shrouded Paul in these years when he was in and out of hospitals; spiritually he was the same, but he regretted that he could only observe world affairs and could not participate.

The world was slowly changing, however. It made a dramatic gesture on the occasion of his seventy-fifth birthday: a "cultural salute" at Carnegie Hall. The dramatic story of Robeson's struggle was depicted in films, slides, and recordings; a number of Broadway and Hollywood names clambered onto Carnegie's stage to pay tribute to him. Evidently, Paul was ecstatic at home in Philadelphia, when he heard the tape of the affair. Somehow his enormous belief in the goodness of people, in ideas that would bring out that "goodness," seemed vindicated. But this new fame didn't make him stop avoiding the public entirely—some say a decision helped along by an overprotective son.

Asked by an intimate about his decision to totally preserve his privacy, Paul replied in the fall of 1975: "People should understand that when I could be active I went here and there and everywhere. What I wanted to do I did; what I wanted to say I said, and now that ill health has compelled my retirement I have decided to let the record speak for itself. As far as my basic outlook is concerned, everybody should know that I'm the same Paul Robeson and the viewpoint that I expressed in my book, *Here I Stand*, has never changed."[5]

The week before Thanksgiving 1975 Ernestine Thomas, a cousin, visited Paul. "He got up, got dressed and came downstairs, and talked about old times. His sister said he didn't do that often."[6]

A few weeks later, on December 28, 1975, Paul was admitted to Presbyterian University Hospital in Philadelphia for treatment of a mild stroke. Tests showed he was suffering from cerebral vascular disorders, and his condition swiftly grew worse. He died on January 23, 1976, at the age of seventy-seven.

Standing in silent appreciation for Paul Robeson at the "Cultural Salute," April 15, 1973 (left to right): Roscoe Lee Brown, Leon Bibb, Zero Mostel, James Earl Jones, Ruby Dee, Sidney Poitier

Epilogue

They came in a steady stream to pay their final respects—old ladies with flowered plastic bags, black men with attaché cases, young blacks and whites in denim. Sitting in the modest Harlem funeral home, they heard the voice of Paul Robeson singing "Ol' Man River" and they said goodbye, as if to an old friend, to the man who had circled the globe with his artistry and his activism.

The funeral was held on January 29, with thousands of people crowding into the Mother A.M.E. Church that had provided a forum for Paul when concert halls were closed to him. Dr. Samuel Rosen, now white-haired, recalled how Paul had given him his first insight into struggle. Bishop J. Clinton Hoggard took up that theme and talked about Paul's strength. The final eulogy was spoken by Paul Robeson, Jr., who concluded with a poem a friend had composed a day earlier: "I may keep memories of him, but not his essence . . . for that will pour forth tomorrow. . . ."

On the day that Paul would have celebrated his seventy-eighth birthday Paul, Jr., announced his father's gravesite, ending a two-month speculation. He and Essie would be buried side by side at Ferncliff Cemetery in Hartsdale, New York. Paul's plaque was inscribed with the words he spoke on a June day in 1937, when his heart was stirred by the Spanish Civil War: "The artist must elect to fight for freedom or for slavery. I have made my choice. I had no alternative."

Notes

Chapter I. Father and Son

1. Edwin Grant Conklin, "As a Scientist Saw Him" quoted in *Woodrow Wilson: Some Princeton Memories*, ed. William Starr Myers (Princeton: Princeton University Press, 1946), p. 52.

2. Arthur Evans Wood, *Some Unsolved Problems of a University Town*, Dissertation, University of Pennsylvania, 1920.

3. "Annual Catalog for the Academical (sic) Year." Lincoln University. Philadelphia, 1873.

4. Paul Robeson, *Here I Stand* (Boston: Beacon Press, 1971), p. 6.

5. *Ibid.*, pp. 11-12.

6. *Ibid.*, p. 6.

7. Eslanda Goode Robeson, *Paul Robeson, Negro* (New York: Harper & Brothers, 1930), p. 161.

8. Douglas J. Brown, "Paul Robeson, the Man," a speech delivered during the Robeson Tribute at Somerville (New Jersey) High, 1973.

9. Paul Robeson, *op. cit.*, p. 21.

10. *Ibid.*, p. 25.

Chapter II. All-American

1. Robert Van Gelder, "Robeson Remembers, An Interview with the Star of *Othello*," *The New York Times*, January 16, 1944.

2. Spoken by Samuel Rosen at Paul Robeson's funeral, January 29, 1976.

3. Marie Seton, *Paul Robeson* (London: Dennis Dobson, 1958), p. 22.

4. *Daily Home News*, June 5, 1919.

Chapter III. Home to Harlem

1. Daniel J. Loeb, *From Sambo to Superspade, The Black Experience in Motion Pictures* (Boston: Houghton-Mifflin Co., 1975), p. 34.

2. *Ibid.*, p. 37.

3. *Daily Home News*, October 16, 1919.

4. John Hope Franklin, *From Slavery to Freedom* (New York: Vintage Books, 1969), p. 478.

5. William O. Douglas, *Go East Young Man: The Early Years* (New York: Random House, 1974), p. 136.

6. From an interview with William O. Douglas, February 1976.

7. From an interview with William L. Patterson, February 1976.

8. Eslanda Robeson, *op. cit.*, p. 70.

9. Seton, *op. cit.*, p. 24.

10. *Ibid.*, p. 9.

11. *Ibid.*, p. 12.

12. *Ibid.*, p. 25.

13. Eslanda Robeson, *op. cit.*, p. 73.

14. *Ibid.*, p. 75.

15. Seton, *op. cit.*, p. 26.

Chapter IV. Enter Eugene O'Neill

1. Barbara and Arthur Gelb, *O'Neill* (New York: Dell Publishing Co., 1962), pp. 449-450.

2. Seton, *op. cit.*, p. 26.

3. Louis Sheaffer, *O'Neill, Son and Artist* (Boston: Little, Brown and Co, 1973), p. 139.

4. W. E. B. Du Bois, "The Negro and Our Stage," in *Provincetown Playbill, 1923-1924 Season*, No. 4.

5. Sheaffer, *op. cit.*, p. 37.

6. *Ibid.*

7. *Ibid.*, p. 143.

8. Thomas Crippes, "Paul Robeson and Black Identity in American Movies," *The Massachusetts Review* (Summer 1970), p. 472.

9. Donald Bogle, *Toms, Coons, Mulattoes, Mammies and Bucks* (New York: The Viking Press, 1973), p. 138.

10. Ben Sidran, *Black Talk* (New York: Holt, Rinehart and Winston, 1971), p. 68.

Chapter V. Ascent to Fame

1. Paul Robeson, "Reflections on O'Neill's Plays," *Opportunities* (December 1924) 2: 368-369.

2. Seton, *op. cit.*, p. 40.

3. Edward Scobie, *Black Britannia* (Chicago: Johnson Publishing Co., 1972), p. 179.

4. Eslanda Robeson, *op. cit.*, p. 106.

5. Frank Lenz, "When Robeson Sings," *Association Men* (July 1927), p. 496.

6. Quoted in Hannen Swaffer's *Who's Who*, October 27, 1928.

7. Hannen Swaffer, "London as It Looks," quoted in *Variety*, October 17, 1928.

8. John Unterecker, *Voyager: A Life of Hart Crane* (New York: Farrar, Straus and Giroux, 1969), p. 576.

9. Seton, *op. cit.*, p. 47.

10. *Ibid.*

11. A. J. P. Taylor, *Beaverbrook* (New York: Simon and Schuster, 1972), p. 235.

12. Kenneth Young, ed., *Diaries of Sir Robert Lockhart* (London: St. Martin's Press, 1973).

13. Seton, *op. cit.*, p. 48.

Chapter VI. A Marriage in Trouble

1. Interview with an old acquaintance who asked not to be identified.

2. *New York Amsterdam News*, October 26, 1932.

3. Correspondence with Marie Seton, April 3, 1976.

4. Eslanda Robeson, *op. cit.*, p. 142.

5. *Morning Post* (London), May 21, 1930.

6. *New York Herald Tribune*, June 1930.

7. Maurice Brown, *Too Late to Lament* (Bloomington: Indiana University Press, 1956), p. 323.

8. *New York Herald Tribune*, June 1930.

9. *Evening News* (London), February 13, 1930.

10. Bryher (nee Winnifred Ellerman), *The Heart of Artemis* (London: Collins, St. James Place, 1963), p. 264.

11. Quoted in Alexander Woollcott, "Ol' Man River in Person," *Hearst's International Cosmopolitan*, July 1933, p. 102.

12. *New York Times*, June 26, 1932.

13. Correspondence with Marie Seton, April 3, 1976.

14. *Chicago Defender*, February 11, 1933; *New York Amsterdam News*, February 1933.

Chapter VII. New Influences

1. Richard Drinnon, *Rebel in Paradise: A Biography of Emma Goldman* (Chicago: University of Chicago Press, 1961), p. 274.

2. *Ibid.*

3. Ronald Adam, *Overture and Beginners* (London: Gollancz, Ltd., 1938), p. 102.

4. Nathan Krans, *The Jewish Transcript*, November 22, 1935.

5. Seton, *op. cit.*, p. 67.

6. *Ibid.*, p. 68.

7. Mortimer Franklin, "Art in Astoria," in *Screenland*, October 1933.

8. Edmund David Gronon, *Black Moses* (Madison: University of Wisconsin Press, 1964), p. 163.

9. *Film Weekly*, September 1, 1933.

10. Murray Kempton, *Part of Our Time* (New York: Simon and Schuster, 1955), p. 247.

11. James R. Hooker, *Black Revolutionary: George Padmore's Path from Communism to Pan Africanism* (New York: Praeger, 1967), p. 28.

12. *Glasgow Citizen*, May 1, 1934.

13. Seton, *op. cit.*, p. 74.

14. Eslanda Robeson, *African Journey* (New York: John Day), p. 14.

15. Seton, *op. cit.*, p. 78.

Chapter VIII. Russia—"For the First Time . . ."

1. Seton, *op. cit.*, pp. 81-85.

2. *Ibid.*, p. 84.

3. Langston Hughes, *I Wonder as I Wander* (New York: Rinehart and Co., 1956), p. 77.

4. Homer Smith, *Black Man in Red Russia* (Chicago: Johnson Publishing Co., 1964), p. 29.

5. Seton, *op. cit.*, p. 87.

6. *Ibid.*, p. 92.

7. Seton, *Sergei M. Eisenstein* (New York: Grove Press, 1960), p. 328.

Chapter IX. Birth of a Political Artist

1. Jeremy Murray-Brown, *Kenyatta* (New York: E. P. Dutton, 1973), p. 216.

2. Crippes, *op. cit.*, p. 480.

3. Seton, *op. cit.*, p. 96.

4. *Daily Worker*, May 1936.

5. Adam, *op. cit.*, p. 145.

6. *Ibid.*

7. *The New York Times*, August 17, 1938, quoted in Crippes, *op. cit.*, p. 482.

8. Harold Cruse, *The Crisis of the Negro Intellectual* (New York: William Morrow, 1967), p. 177.

9. Clarence G. Contee, quoted in "Black American 'Reds' and African Liberation: A Case Study of the Council on African Affairs, 1937-1955," ed. Lorraine A. Williams, *Proceedings—The Conference on Afro-Americans and Africans: Historical and Political Linkages* (Washington, D.C.: The Graduate School of Howard University, 1975), pp. 117-133.

10. Paul Robeson, *op. cit.*, p. 52.

11. Horace R. Cayton, *Long Old Road* (New York: Trident Press, 1965), pp. 241-242.

12. Poppy Cannon, *A Gentle Knight: My Husband Walter White* (New York: Rinehart, 1956), p. 269.

Chapter X. Ballad for Americans

1. Seton, *op. cit.*, p. 127.

2. Virginia Hamilton, *Paul Robeson: The Life and Times of a Free Black Man* (New York: Harper & Row, 1974), p. 88.

3. Helen Arstein and Carlton Moss, *Lena Horne* (New York: Greenberg, 1950).

4. *San Francisco Chronicle*, September 23, 1942.

5. Michel Fabre, *The Unfinished Quest of Richard Wright* (New York: William Morrow, 1973), p. 237.

Chapter XI. The Moor

1. Seton, *op. cit.*, p. 150.

2. *Ibid.*

3. Stark Young, *The New Republic*, November 1, 1943.

4. Seton, *op. cit.*, p. 154.

5. An article in the *Cleveland Plain Dealer* by William McDermott, quoted in Norman Nadel, *A Pictorial History of the Theatre Guild* (New York: Crown Publishers, 1969), pp. 184-186.

Chapter XII. Riding High

1. Contee, *op. cit.*

2. Interview with Stanley D. Levinson, March 24, 1975.

3. In correspondence with Claire Polakoff, niece of Olga Gow, May-June 1976.

4. Interview with Mason Roberson, 1975.

5. *The Chicago Defender*, October 28, 1944.

6. Walter White, *A Rising Wind*, quoted in Gilbert Osofsky, *The Burden of Race* (New York: Harper & Row, 1967).

Chapter XIII. Cold Warrior

1. Paul Robeson, *op. cit.*, p. 40.

2. Seton, *op. cit.*, p. 169.

3. Wilson Record, *The Negro and the Communist Party* (Chapel Hill: The University of North Carolina Press, 1951), p. 254.

Chapter XIV. Progressive Politics

1. Interview with Dr. Al McQueen, professor, Oberlin College, September 1975.

2. *The New York Times*, June 1, 1948.

Chapter XV. Paris Aftermath

1. Letters from the Department of Justice, Washington, D.C.

2. Seton, *op. cit.*, p. 199.

3. *Ibid.*, p. 201.

4. Interview with an old acquaintance of Paul Robeson, Jr.

5. Hearings in the U.S. House of Representatives, regarding Communist Infiltration of Minority Groups, July 1-3, 14, 18, 1949.

6. Carl Rowan, "Has Paul Robeson Betrayed the Negro?" *Ebony Magazine* (July 1957), p. 38.

Chapter XVI. An Artist Besieged

1. For the description of the first concert I have relied in part on Howard Fast, *Peekskill: U.S.A.: A Personal Experience* (The Civil Rights Congress, 1951).

2. Dr. Henry Atkinson *et al.*, *Violence in Peekskill* (American Civil Liberties Union).

3. Westchester Committee for a Fair Inquiry into the Peekskill Violence, "Eyewitness: Peekskill USA."

4. "Peekskill and Germany," in "Letters to the Editor," *The Nation* (September 1949) 11, No. 12, p. 2.

5. Interview with Harold Marcus, February 4, 1976.

6. Westchester Committee for a Fair Inquiry into the Peekskill Violence, *op. cit.*

7. *The Peekskill Star*, September 6, 1949.

8. Atkinson *et al.*, *op. cit.*

Chapter XVII. Prisoner in His Own Land

1. James Aronson, *The Press and the Cold War* (New York: Bobbs-Merrill, 1970), p. 55.

2. Albert E. Kahn, *High Treason*, quoted in Aronson, *op. cit.*

3. Interview with journalist Ray Rogers, October 1975.

4. Seton, *op. cit.*, p. 143.

5. Interviews with an old Robeson acquaintance who asked not to be identified, 1974-1975.

6. Correspondence with Marie Seton, April 3, 1976.

7. Interview with Julian Mayfield, August 1975.

Chapter XVIII. "Are You Now . . .?"

1. Robeson did not attend the University of Pennsylvania.

2. Paul Robeson, Jr., spent two years in a Soviet grammar school and graduated from Cornell University.

Chapter XIX. Free at Last

1. Interview with John Oliver Killens, February 1976.

2. Hy Kraft, *On My Way to the Theater* (New York: Macmillan, Inc., 1971), pp. 164-165.

3. Konstantin Kudrov, "A Russian Remembrance," *Rutgers Alumni Magazine* (Winter 1975), p. 27.

4. *Ibid.*

5. Interview with Lloyd L. Brown, recounted publicly by Brown on February 4, 1976.

6. Interview with Ernestine Thomas, January 29, 1976.

Bibliography

Adam, Ronald. *Overture and Beginners*. London: Gollancz, Ltd., 1938.

Allen, Frederick Lewis. *Only Yesterday*. New York: Bantam Books, 1959.

Anderson, Marian. *My Lord, What a Morning*. New York: The Viking Press, 1956.

Aptheker, Herbert (ed.). *Annotated Bibliography of the Published Writings of W. E. B. Du Bois*. Millwood, New York: Kraus-Thomson Organization Limited, 1973.

Aronson, James. *The Press and the Cold War*. Indianapolis: The Bobbs-Merrill Co., Inc., 1970.

Arstein, Helen, and Moss, Carlton. *Lena Horne*. New York: Greenberg, 1950.

Atkinson, Henry, *et. al. Violence in Peekskill*. American Civil Liberties Union.

Barbour, Floyd B. (ed.). *The Black Seventies*. Boston: Porter Sargent, 1970.

Bentley, Eric (ed.). *Thirty Years of Treason: Excerpts from Hearings Before the House Committee on Un-American Activities, 1938-1968*. New York: The Viking Press, 1972.

Bogle, Donald. *Toms, Coons, Mulattoes, Mammies, and Bucks: An Interpretive History of Blacks in American Films*. New York: The Viking Press, 1973.

Brockway, Archibald Fenner. *Inside the Left: Thirty Years of Platform, Press, Prison and Parliament*. London: George Allen and Unwin, Ltd., 1947.

Browne, Maurice. *Too Late to Lament*. Bloomington, Ind.: Indiana University Press, 1956.

Cannon, Poppy. *A Gentle Knight: My Husband Walter White*. New York: Rinehart and Co., Inc., 1956.

Cayton, Horace R. *Long Old Road*. New York: Trident Press, 1965.

Collins, V. Lansing. *Princeton, Past and Present*. Princeton, N.J.: Princeton University Press, 1931.

Cronon, Edmund David. *Black Moses: the Story of Marcus Garvey and the Universal Negro Improvement Association*. Madison, Wisconsin: The University of Wisconsin Press, 1964.

Cruse, Harold. *The Crisis of the Negro Intellectual*. New York: William Morrow and Company, Inc., 1967.

David, Jay (ed.). *Growing Up Black*. New York: Pocket Books, 1969.

Douglas, William O. *Go East Young Man: The Early Years*. New York: Random House, 1974.

Draper, Theodore. *The Roots of American Communism*. New York: The Viking Press, 1957.

Drinnon, Richard. *Rebel in Paradise: A Biography of Emma Goldman*. Chicago: University of Chicago Press, 1961.

Du Bois, W. E. Burghardt. *The Souls of Black Folk*. Greenwich, Conn.: Fawcett Publications, Inc., 1961.

Ellison, Ralph. *Invisible Man*. Harmondsworth, Middlesex, England: Penguin Books, Ltd., 1965.

Fabre, Michel. *The Unfinished Quest of Richard Wright*. New York: William Morrow, 1973.

Fast, Howard Melvin. *Peekskill: USA: A Personal Experience*. n.p.: The Civil Rights Congress, 1951.

Ferguson, Blanche E. *Countee Cullen and the Negro Renaissance*. New York: Dodd, Mead and Co., 1966.

Franklin, John Hope. *From Slavery to Freedom: A History of Negro Americans*. 3rd ed. New York: Vintage Books, 1969.

Gelb, Arthur, and Barbara. *O'Neill*. New York: Dell Publishing Co., 1962.

Gilmore, Al-Tony. *Bad Nigger: the National Impact of Jack Johnson*. Port Washington, New York: Kennikat Press, 1975.

Graham, Shirley. *Paul Robeson: Citizen of the World*. New York: Julian Messner, Inc., 1971.

Hamilton, Virginia. *Paul Robeson: the Life and Times of a Free Black Man.* New York: Harper & Row, 1974.

Hansberry, Lorraine. *To Be Young, Gifted and Black.* New York: The New American Library, Inc., 1970.

Helm, MacKinley. *Angel Mo' and her Son, Roland Hayes.* Boston: Little, Brown and Co., 1942.

Hentoff, Nat. *The New Equality.* New York: The Viking Press, 1964.

Herndon, Angelo. *Let Me Live.* New York: Arno Press and the New York Times, 1969.

Hooker, James R. *Black Revolutionary: George Padmore's Path from Communism to Pan-Africanism.* New York: Praeger Publishers, 1967.

Howe, Irving, and Coser, Lewis. *The American Communist Party: A Critical History (1919-1957).* Boston: Beacon Press, 1957.

Hoyt, Edwin Palmer. *Paul Robeson: The American Othello.* Cleveland: The World Publishing Co., 1967.

Huggins, Nathan Irwin. *Harlem Renaissance.* New York: Oxford University Press, 1971.

Hughes, Langston. *Fight for Freedom: The Story of the NAACP.* New York: Berkley Publishing Co., 1962.

   I Wonder As I Wander: An Autobiographical Journey. New York: Rinehart and Co., Inc., 1956.

Johnson, James Weldon, and Johnson, J. Rosamund (eds.). *The Book of American Negro Spirituals.* New York: The Viking Press, 1969.

Katz, William Loren. *Eyewitness: The Negro in American History.* 3rd ed. New York: Pitman Publishing Corporation, 1974.

Kempton, Murray. *Part of Our Time: Some Ruins and Monuments of the Thirties.* New York: Simon and Schuster, 1955.

Kraft, Hy. *On My Way to the Theater.* New York: Macmillan, Inc. 1971.

Krems, Nathan. *The Jewish Transcript.* November 22, 1935.

Lacy, Leslie Alexander. *The Rise and Fall of a Proper Negro.* New York: Macmillan, Inc., 1970.

Landay, Eileen. *Black Film Stars.* New York: Drake Publishers, Inc., 1973.

Leab, Daniel J. *From Sambo to Superspade: The Black Experience in Motion Pictures*. Boston: Houghton Mifflin Company, 1975.

Lewis, Thomas S.W. (ed.). *Letters of Hart Crane and His Family*. New York: Columbia University Press, 1974.

Logan, Rayford W., and Cohen, Irving S. *The American Negro: Old World Background and New World Experience*. Boston: Houghton Mifflin Company, 1967.

Masuoka, Jitsuichi, and Valien, Preston (eds.). *Race Relations: Problems and Theory*. Chapel Hill, North Carolina: The University of North Carolina Press, 1961.

Meir, August, Rudwick, Elliott, and Broderick, Francis L. (eds.). *Black Protest Thought in the Twentieth Century*. 2nd ed. Indianapolis: The Bobbs-Merrill Co., Inc., 1965.

Miers, Earl Schenck. *Big Ben*. Philadelphia: The Westminster Press, 1942.

Morris, Lloyd. *Incredible New York: High Life and Low Life of the Last Hundred Years*. New York: Random House, 1951.

Murray-Brown, Jeremy. *Kenyatta*. New York: E.P. Dutton and Co., Inc., 1973.

Myers, William Starr (ed.). *Woodrow Wilson: Some Princeton Memories*. Princeton, New Jersey: Princeton University Press, 1946.

Nadel, Norman. *A Pictorial History of the Theatre Guild*. New York: Crown Publishers, Inc., 1969.

The Norton Facsimile: The First Folio of Shakespeare. Prepared by Charles Hinman. New York: W.W. Norton and Co., Inc., 1968.

Osofsky, Gilbert. *The Burden of Race*. New York: Harper & Row, 1967.

Parsons, Talcott, and Clark, Kenneth B. (eds.). *The American Negro*. Boston: Beacon Press, 1967.

Patterson, Lindsay (ed.). *Black Films and Film-Makers*. New York: Dodd, Mead and Company, 1975.

Paul Robeson: The Great Forerunner, A Special Issue of *Freedomways*. 1st quarter. New York: Freedomways Associates, Inc., 1971.

Podhoretz, Norman. *Making It*. New York: Bantam Books, 1969.

Record, Wilson. *The Negro and the Communist Party*. Chapel Hill, North Carolina: The University of North Carolina Press, 1951.

Richardson, Ben. *Great American Negroes*. New York: Thomas Y. Crowell Co., 1945.

Robeson, Eslanda Goode. *African Journey*. New York: The John Day Co., 1945.

  Paul Robeson, Negro. New York: Harper & Brothers, 1930.

Robeson, Paul. *Here I Stand*. Boston: Beacon Press, 1971.

Rowan, Carl T. *Just Between Us Blacks*. New York: Random House, 1974.

Schlosser, Anatol I. *Paul Robeson: His Career in the Theatre, in Motion Pictures, and on the Concert Stage*. Ph.D. dissertation, School of Education, New York University, 1970. Facsimile produced by Xerox University Microfilms, Ann Arbor, Michigan, 1974.

Scobie, Edward. *Black Britannia: A History of Blacks in Britain*. Chicago: Johnson Publishing Co., Inc., 1972.

Seton, Marie. *Paul Robeson*. London: Dennis Dobson, 1958.

  Sergei M. Eisenstein. New York: Grove Press, Inc., 1960.

Sheaffer, Louis. *O'Neill: Son and Artist*. Boston: Little, Brown and Co., 1973.

Sidran, Ben. *Black Talk*. New York: Holt, Rinehart and Winston, 1971.

Smith, Homer. *Black Man in Red Russia*. Chicago: Johnson Publishing Co., 1964.

Southern, Eileen. *The Music of Black Americans: A History*. New York: W.W. Norton and Co., Inc., 1971.

Starobin, Joseph Robert. *Eyewitness in Indo-China*. New York: Greenwood Press, 1968.

Stone, Isidor F. *The Hidden History of the Korean War*. New York: Monthly Review Press, 1952.

Taylor, A.J.P. *Beaverbrook*. New York: Simon and Schuster, 1972.

This Is Our War. Baltimore: The Afro-American Co., 1945.

Thomas, Hugh. *John Strachey*. New York: Harper & Row, 1973.

Walden, Daniel (ed.). *W.E.B. Du Bois: The Crisis Writings*. Greenwich, Conn.: Fawcett Publications, Inc., 1972.

Weaver, Harold D. "Paul Robeson: Beleaguered Leader," *The Black Scholar*, V., No. 4 (December 1973-January 1974).

Weyand, Alexander. *The Saga of American Football*. New York: Macmillan, Inc., 1955.

White, Walter Francis. *A Man Called White*. New York: Arno Press and the New York Times, 1969.

White, William Allen. *A Puritan in Babylon: The Story of Calvin Coolidge*. New York: Capricorn Books, 1965.

Williams, John A., and Harris, Charles F. (eds.). *Amistad 2: Writings on Black History and Culture*. New York: Vintage Books, 1971.

Williams, Lorraine (ed.). *Proceedings—The Conference on Afro-Americans and Africans: Historical and Political Linkages*. Washington, D.C.: The Graduate School of Howard University, 1975.

Yette, Samuel F. *The Choice: The Issue of Black Survival in America*. New York: G.P. Putnam's Sons, 1971.

Robeson Plays

Simon the Cyrenian	
Taboo/Voodoo	1922
All God's Chillun Got Wings	1924
The Emperor Jones	1924
Black Boy	1926
Porgy	1927
Show Boat	1928
Othello	1930
The Hairy Ape	1931
Show Boat (Revival)	1932
All God's Chillun Got Wings (London Production)	1933
Basalik	1935
Stevedore	1935
Toussaint L'Ouverture	1936
Unity Theatre: Plant in the Sun	1938
The Emperor Jones (Revival)	1939
John Henry	1939
Revivals: Show Boat and The Emperor Jones	1940
Othello	1942
Othello	1959

Films

Borderline	1930
The Emperor Jones	1933
Sanders of the River	1935

Index

Composed in Palatino by The New Republic Book
Company, Inc., Washington, D.C.

Printed and bound by Halliday Lithograph, Hanover,
Massachusetts.

Designed by Gerard Valerio.